WORDS &
DEEDS

The Achievements of
Governor George V. Voinovich

WORDS &
DEEDS

The Achievements of
Governor George V. Voinovich

Florence Clark Riffe

OHIO UNIVERSITY SPECIAL PUBLICATIONS

ATHENS

ISBN 0-9667644-0-4 (pbk.: alk. paper)

CONTENTS

FOREWORD

by Curt Steiner, Chief of Staff

IN MARCH 1989, I traveled to Cleveland to meet with a fellow Ohio University graduate who was serving what turned out to be his tenth and final year as mayor of Cleveland. The purpose of my meeting with George Voinovich was to discuss his possible entry into the coming 1990 campaign for governor of Ohio, as well as my potential involvement in a Voinovich candidacy. At that early point in the process, many political observers believed Mr. Voinovich's prospects were bleak.

Accordingly, our conversation was a candid one. There was no shortage of reasons for him *not* to enter the race, and I made sure we discussed all of them. He was barely four months removed from an Election Day trouncing by Howard Metzenbaum in the 1988 campaign for United States Senate. Many pundits viewed his devastating defeat as the end of George Voinovich as a statewide candidate. His campaign war chest was empty. Even some of his friends were encouraging him to lay low for awhile and allow more time for the memories of his ill-fated Senate campaign to fade.

The man I encountered that day, however, was one who had already made up his mind. George Voinovich was running for governor. It simply did not matter to him that his campaign coffers were dry, or that his political epitaph (at least in some quarters) was already written. He did not care that prominent Republicans were already being mentioned as probable candidates, or that Democrat opposition likely would be formidable.

Mr. Voinovich had considered all of this. First and foremost, he was certain his qualifications would stack up against anyone's. He talked about his methodical management style and inclusive leadership philosophy, which had helped bring about the "Cleveland comeback" during that decade. Mr. Voinovich felt those attributes would appeal to voters in a state whose economic engine was sputtering and whose financial condition was worsening. With a winning message, money could, *of course*, be raised for the governor's race. His northeast Ohio base remained strong, if somewhat weakened by his recent defeat. He was anxious to begin assembling a crackerjack campaign team.

During that meeting, I began to recognize the character traits that define George Voinovich. A calm confidence. A thoughtful, analytical approach to addressing every challenge. A dogged determination—indeed, a stubborn insistence—to stay the course once a decision was made. A deep faith in God. A fire in his belly that lit a contagious strain of courage. Indeed, George Voinovich had what it took to win a tough campaign and become a great governor.

I made up my mind on the spot. Within days, I resigned my post as communications director for the Ohio Republican Senate caucus and signed on to help run the Voinovich for Governor campaign. In April 1989, George Voinovich announced his candidacy, and off we went.

A year and a half later, in November 1990, Mr. Voinovich was elected Ohio's sixty-fifth governor and in 1994 was reelected with 72 percent of the vote. His victory margin in 1994 was a twentieth-century Ohio record, and the largest in the nation by a Republican candidate for governor that year.

This book is intended as a straightforward presentation of some of what was accomplished in the eight years of the Voinovich administration. It was written during Governor Voinovich's final weeks in office, when records were still readily accessible and memories still reasonably fresh.

Perhaps unfortunately, this book does *not* attempt to offer a view of the man himself. What made George Voinovich tick as governor?

How did he handle his most serious crises and difficult decisions? What motivated or inspired him? Those questions are left for another chronicler to answer. However, what immediately follows provides at least a glimpse into the soul of the man who led Ohio through most of the final decade of the twentieth century.

Interestingly, the process of writing this book yielded an insight into Governor Voinovich that was as telling as any other might be. During the fall of 1998, the governor was asked to identify the "defining moments" of his administration. It was hoped his answer might produce a little spice for sprinkling upon the otherwise fact-oriented text of this book.

Without much hesitation, he replied that the key defining moment actually occurred in the weeks after his election in 1990 and *before* he took office as governor. It was then, the governor recounted, that he first realized that "people were going to be as willing to help me as governor as they were when I was mayor of Cleveland." An inspired Voinovich immediately began planning the broad array of task forces he would empower to help him reinvent state government and reinvigorate Ohio's economy. Most of these are discussed at length in this book.

His response was vintage Voinovich. Hold the spice, please. The steady, consensus-building, managerial governor instinctively ignored major events and turning points that had commanded huge headlines during his years in office and chose a defining moment that was . . . well, sort of *bland*.

He did not choose the Lucasville prison riot in April 1993, by consensus considered the gravest crisis of Governor Voinovich's tenure. Nine inmates and one guard lost their lives during the eleven-day siege—the longest riot at any state prison in America's history. His handling of the crisis revealed much about the governor, both as an individual and a leader. Some in his position might have opted for a highly public role in managing the crisis—tough talk, photo ops outside the prison walls, and the like.

Not George Voinovich. He did let a long-scheduled trade mission to Eastern Europe take off without him. But he chose to maintain a low profile throughout the period, calling the shots behind the scenes based on the advice of the law enforcement experts who guided negotiations. Tormented in private by fears of far greater loss of life, the governor withstood increasing pressure to storm the prison walls and end the stand-off with force.

In the end, his patient, restrained handling of the disturbance was widely viewed as "textbook," drawing praise from no less an interested party than Democrat House Speaker Vern Riffe, in whose home county the prison is situated. And James J. Hughes, National Guard Commander at Lucasville (and staunch Democrat), had this to say in a letter to the governor written soon after the riot was over: "Governor, this is the 19th riot or other civil disaster that I have participated in, either as a member of the National Guard or as the Safety Director of Columbus during the early 1970's. Your performance as the Commander-in-Chief of the Guard and the Chief Executive Officer of the State was superior and the criticism thereof is without factual basis."

True to form, Governor Voinovich had empowered others to help him set a course of action, which he then maintained with fierce determination. A year earlier, he had done the same when he stood firm behind the decision he and the Ohio General Assembly had made to eliminate General Assistance for able-bodied Ohioans.

The issue came into sharp focus on April 1, 1992, when the turbulent debate surrounding welfare cutbacks roiled into a memorable scene at the State House. That afternoon, the governor held an open—and sometimes heated—meeting in the cabinet room with members of Cleveland City Council who had traveled to Columbus to voice their concerns about welfare reform. Outside, hundreds of protesters vented their anger at the governor with chants of "Hey, ho, George has got to go." Following the meeting, a reporter asked Governor Voinovich what he would say to the people outside. Choking back tears, he replied "I'm doing the best I can with what we've got."

State House cynics publicly suggested the tears were faked. Others thought the governor might be wavering in his decision to go ahead with welfare cutbacks. In fact, the emotion was real and the resolve, steadfast. The devout Voinovich felt deep compassion for Ohio's neediest citizens, and he understood that cutbacks would have an adverse effect on many people in the short term. But he also believed that the course of action he had set was the best for enabling thousands of Ohioans trapped in the welfare cycle to begin the journey toward self-sufficiency. He stayed the course and, today, Ohio is viewed as a model for helping people make the transition from welfare to work.

Other "defining moments" were plentiful during the Voinovich years. For example, driven by his faith and his ever-present desire to protect Ohio families, Governor Voinovich personally led the "crusade" in 1996 to keep casino gambling out of the state.

The discrimination his immigrant grandparents faced instilled in the young George Voinovich a fierce commitment to equal rights. That commitment manifested itself on numerous occasions during his governorship, as witnessed in his determined efforts to save Central State University (Ohio's only predominantly African-American public university) and to preserve the state's minority business program. Further, in 1992, Voinovich convened the first of four "Governor's Challenge" conferences in Columbus. The biannual conferences brought together leaders from Ohio's urban centers to examine ways to foster improved race relations, and featured keynote addresses by some of the nation's preeminent experts on the subject. An old friend of the governor's, Coretta Scott King, participated in the inaugural conference in 1992.

Other aspects of his own family life contributed to the governor's decision to "draw a line in the sand" and make the health and education of Ohio's children his top priority as governor. In a videotape produced for the governor's Family and Children First Initiative, he recounted the story of how his father and an uncle were orphaned as children. His father was eventually adopted by a loving foster family and led a long and successful life. But his uncle "got lost in the cracks . . . he didn't have the love, didn't have the family." The uncle eventually died in the streets, homeless. Years later, the memory of his uncle still served as an inspiration to George Voinovich to do "everything I can to make a difference in the lives of our children."

Indeed, the Voinovich years were punctuated with more than a few moments of high drama, as well as many other examples of political courage, rock-solid resolve, and genuine love for his fellow man. Future students of history may well label those as the defining moments of Governor Voinovich's time in office. But the man, himself, would always recall his finest hours as those when he empowered others to get involved and make a difference.

My biases aside, I sincerely believe that George Voinovich's two terms in office will stand up very well in Ohio history. I, myself, was privileged to stand with my fellow Bobcat on the night of November 3, 1998—some forty years after his graduation from Ohio University—as he offered his victory speech upon his election to the United States Senate. The victory made him only the fifteenth person to serve Ohio as both governor and senator, and certainly affirmed the affection and regard his contemporaries felt for him.

Even in a moment of such exultant accomplishment, the governor eschewed soaring rhetoric and chose, instead, the familiar rhythms from so many speeches over so many years of public service. He said: "On a night like this, one experiences many emotions, but I can quickly identify the one that Janet and I feel most vividly—and it's gratitude. . . . I'm grateful for the privilege I've been given to serve the people of Ohio for these last eight years and for the opportunity to make a positive difference in the lives of our fellow citizens."

Vintage Voinovich.

Curt Steiner is a 1978 graduate of Ohio University. From 1989 through 1998, Steiner served George Voinovich in numerous capacities in and out of government. From 1996 through 1998, he was Governor Voinovich's chief of staff.

WORDS &
DEEDS

The Achievements of
Governor George V. Voinovich

CHAPTER 1

Together We Did It

"I believe government's highest calling is to empower people and galvanize their energy and resources to help solve our problems, meet our challenges, and seize our opportunities. I also believe it's a leader's role to reach deep into every individual, draw out the goodness that's inside, and inspire people to use that goodness to help themselves, their families, and their communities."

EMPOWER IS HIS favorite word. Ohio Governor George Voinovich can't talk about his achievements without using the word, and using it often. He's empowered people formerly accustomed to dependency to return to the self-satisfaction of self-sufficiency. He's empowered people to help children to start life in a better position to develop their talents. He's empowered state employees to work harder and smarter by making them partners in the quest for continuous improvement of the state's services. And he's empowered employers and employees alike to thrive in Ohio's new pro-business climate, where the forecast calls for measurable amounts of new jobs. Ask him to name what he considers his most significant

1

achievement in eight years as governor of the nation's seventh largest state and he'll say, "Empowering people—making them aware that they are stewards of energy, knowledge, and virtue that have value only when those talents are spent."

The beginning of the story of how he empowered the people of a state will be marked by historians as January 14, 1991, Inauguration Day. But he alluded to the real beginning in the third paragraph of his speech that day: "It's hard to believe that I'm standing here this morning in front of the Capitol, the grandson of immigrants, a kid from the east side of Cleveland who dreamed that, one day, he might become governor. Today that dream comes true." The journey from Cleveland's Collinwood neighborhood to the Statehouse in Columbus took work beyond mere duty, unyielding tenacity, compatibility with his fellow humans that puts him at their service, and a sense of stewardship honed by family and church. The story of what one trusted aide calls the "infectious commitment" of Governor Voinovich begins long before 1991.

"A kid from the east side of Cleveland"

Under the heading "Previous Experience" on his resume before 1991 were the entries Mayor of Cleveland, Lieutenant Governor, State Legislator, Cuyahoga County Commissioner, Cuyahoga County Auditor, and Assistant Ohio Attorney General. Though the jobs in city, county, and state government surely prepared him to be governor, they in little way explain his passion for governing. He told Ohioans in his second Inaugural Address, "I believe government's highest calling is to empower people and galvanize their energy and resources to help solve our problems, meet our challenges, and seize our opportunities. I also believe it's a leader's role to reach deep into every individual, draw out the goodness that's inside, and inspire people to use that goodness to help themselves, their families, and their communities." He said that belief was instilled in him by his parents, who taught him "that part of earning and deserving our citizenship was giving back, not only to our immediate family, but to our community and to our country."

"Earning and deserving our citizenship"

The parents who taught him the essence of service were George S. Voinovich, a first-generation American whose Serbian parents had immigrated from northern Yugoslavia, and Josephine Bernot Voinovich, whose parents had come to America from Slovenia. A story the governor told about his father in his first Inaugural Address sheds light on the family philosophy of how one person can assuredly make a difference in the life of another. When his father was sixteen, the uncle who had adopted him urged the youth to quit school and take a laborer's job. "The principal of the high school, Mr. Findlay, and a history teacher, Pop Shriver, helped him find a job in an architect's office at night," the governor recounted. "Dad went on to graduate from high school, receive a Kroger's Scholarship to Carnegie Tech, become an architect, president of the Architects' Society of Ohio and chairman of the state architects' Board of Examiners. Until the day he died in 1974, the pictures of those two men who made a difference in his life hung on his office wall."

It was his mother's turn for praise in the second Inaugural Address when he held her up as an example of selfless service. "One such person is my own mother, who, although in her eighties, still worked as a volunteer in the library of an inner city school. My brothers and sisters and I would ask her, 'Mom, why are you doing this? You've done enough! Why don't you just rest and take it easy?' Her answer was always the same. 'Because I'm needed.'" The story was told to encourage Ohioans to volunteer, to convince them they could make a difference in others' lives, but it also revealed the foundation of Governor Voinovich's philosophy of using one's talents to help others.

George Victor Voinovich was born July 15, 1936, the oldest of six children, all of whom caught the fervor for social commitment from their parents. Civic clubs, scouts, PTAs, and churches are some of the organizations that have benefited from three generations of dedication from American Voinovichs. Even when they played, the family spent time together nurturing their unity. It was on a family car trip to Southeastern Ohio when George was thirteen years old that he first visited Athens and Ohio University, the oldest public university northwest of the Ohio River. "I knew then I wanted to go to Ohio

University for college," he said, making a promise to himself he kept five years later. While at Collinwood High School, he served as president of the Key Club, an arm of Kiwanis International, and got to sample leadership as a means to render service to others. His senior year his classmates elected George Voinovich class president. Other presidencies to his credit are president of East Green Council and president of the student body in 1958–59 at Ohio University, where he majored in government, and president of his graduating class at The Ohio State University School of Law. Among the other organizations that have elected him leader are the National Governors' Association, which he served as chair in 1997–98, and the National League of Cities, which he served as president in 1985. He is the only person to have headed both the governors' and cities' organizations.

When Voinovich finished law school in 1961, he followed his plan of returning to Collinwood to practice law. The next year he married Janet Allan, whom he had met while they were campaigning for the same mayoral candidate in Cleveland in 1959. In 1963 he got his first opportunity at state service as an Assistant Attorney General, heading the trial section of the Bureau of Workman's Compensation, as it was called in those days.

In a classic example of the phenomenon that people will cross party lines to vote for a popular candidate, the voters of Collinwood elected Republican candidate George Voinovich to the Ohio House of Representatives in 1966. He was elected to two more terms from the district in which Democrats outnumbered Republicans six to one. As sponsor or cosponsor, Representative Voinovich affixed his name to eighty-five bills that became law during five years in Columbus. In 1971 he was appointed Cuyahoga County Auditor, a position he was elected to twice before running for Cuyahoga County Commissioner. When he won a commission seat in 1976, it marked the first time in more than forty years that Republicans controlled the county's governing body.

All six Voinovichs—George, Janet, George Jr., Peter, Betsy, and Molly—campaigned as a team in 1978 for Dad's election to Lieutenant Governor under Governor James Rhodes. But less than a year later the family was back in Cleveland. Civic leaders, dismayed at the fact that Cleveland had become the first city since the Great Depression to go into default, had asked Voinovich to run for mayor. His campaign slogan, which became a motto that ends most of his speeches to this day, was "Together we can do it"—symbolizing the Voinovich prescription for teamwork that has empowered all his public service.

"Together we can do it."

Again in 1979 the six Voinovichs put up posters, waved signs, and shook hands in a unity reminiscent of the 1978 run. Tragedy was the farthest thing from the minds of the family campaigning for Dad in 1979 when a driver ran a red light in Cleveland. Nine-year-old Molly Voinovich was struck and killed. Friends of the Voinovichs created the Molly Agnes Voinovich Memorial Endowment, the interest on which is distributed annually by the governor and his wife to Oliver Hazard Perry School and to one other Major Works school in Cleveland. The youngest child of George and Janet Voinovich is also remembered half a world away near Yokneam, Israel, in the Molly Voinovich Recreation Area and Forest, where Israeli and Arab children play every day. Though friends and family said the Roman Catholic Church had always been a source of his strength, Voinovich turned even more often to God and prayer after losing Molly. He attends mass more frequently than the obligatory Sunday, even daily when his schedule permits.

In 1990, after serving ten years as mayor of Cleveland, George Voinovich won the governorship he had dreamed about. As the Republican candidate for governor against Democrat and fellow-Clevelander Anthony J. Celebrezze, Jr., Voinovich succeeded Governor Richard Celeste in 1991. What follows within these pages is a record of George Voinovich's accomplishments during eight years in the Governor's Office in Columbus, achieved in partnership with the General Assembly. It examines the key pledges made by the governor in two Inaugural Addresses and eight State of the State Addresses, then follows those words into deeds—actions, policies, law—through the clearer lens of retrospect. Though more pages are devoted to major initiatives, the less heralded accomplishments throughout the state's agency structure are also included.

The chapter outline derives from Governor Voinovich's own vision for making Ohio a better place to live and work, a vision described in the *Ohio 2000/Ohio First* blueprint for action. (1) Management, (2) Jobs and Economic Development, (3) Education, and (4) Quality of Life have been the four aspects of governmental action the governor has emphasized. The chapter on Management focuses on using resources, both human and monetary, more wisely, and on how the Voinovich brand of stewardship was implemented. The discussion of Jobs and Economic Development reviews the efforts of the Voinovich administration to get more people into jobs, to get more jobs into Ohio, and to get more exports out. The category of Education covers everything that fits the definition of instruction—preschool, kindergarten through twelfth grade, post-secondary, and job training. Though Governor Voinovich has repeatedly stressed that improvements in the first three categories all affect Quality of Life, it became a chapter in its own right to detail achievements in health care, the environment, public safety, and consumer protection.

"My thanks go to all who have served in the Ohio General Assembly since 1991 and who contributed to an era of unprecedented bipartisan cooperation on the issues that mattered most."

Absent from the accounting is the daily politicking, cajoling, and sweating demanded by the process of effecting change. Those are interesting and instructive stories, but they are available elsewhere in news media archives or will emerge later in history books. Within those stories, though, are the full details of the role the General Assembly played in bringing to fruition many of the goals Governor Voinovich had set for Ohio. He praised the legislature time and time again, saying in his last State of the State Address, "My thanks go to all who have served in the Ohio General Assembly since 1991 and who contributed to an era of unprecedented bipartisan cooperation on the issues that mattered most."

Within these pages is simply a capsule summary of the accomplishments in state government in the years 1991–98, when a kid from the east side of Cleveland gave something back to his state in order to earn and deserve his citizenship. As Governor Voinovich himself said in his first State of the State Address, "I firmly believe that our stewardship at this critical juncture will chart Ohio's course, not only in the 1990s, but well into the next century."

CHAPTER 2

Management

"Gone are the days when public officials are measured by how much they spend on a problem. The new realities dictate that public officials are now judged on whether they can work harder and smarter, and do more with less."

"I AM A TIGHTWAD."

THERE IS NO BETTER place to start a discussion of Governor George Voinovich's achievements in the arena of management than with his quote, "We must work harder and smarter, and do more with less." He showcased the refrain in both the 1991 and 1995 Inaugural Addresses and eight State of the State Addresses, plus interviews and conversations so numerous that one of his cabinet members dubbed it a mantra. The Voinovich approach, though, has been more than a "get more bang for the buck" cliché. It is a philosophy extolled by the governor who called himself a tightwad in the 1993 State of the State Address and similar epithets in other forums.

He did not ask others to tighten belts without first doing so himself. As the governor said in March 1991, "I'm an ordinary person. As most of you know, I shine my own shoes" and "I don't need the state airplane flown from where it's hangared to my back door, just for the sake of personal convenience." (Two and a half years later he sold the largest of the state's three airplanes traditionally used by Ohio governors.) In the weeks preceding those words, Governor Voinovich had cut his office staff by 17 percent and the staff at his residence by half. Indeed, the fiscal crisis when he took office was so severe that he insisted Ohio make do with maps bearing the likeness of his predecessor, Governor Richard Celeste. Furthermore, the cost of the maps to the state dropped from 26¢ each in 1990 to 7¢ each in 1997.

What was innovative about the Voinovich cost-cutting, though, was that it spread systematically from the governor's office to the agencies on lower floors in the Vern Riffe Center to the Capitol across High Street and into the state beyond the I-270 beltway around Columbus. Equally innovative was the implementation method of his philosophy in a two-step process that brought as many Ohioans as possible into the decision making. Phase One, the Operations Improvement Task Force, called on citizens from the private sector to work with public officials to make recommendations for improving state functions. Phase Two, Quality Services through Partnership, called on rank-and-file state employees to share space at the decision-making table with the people viewed traditionally as the decision makers—the bosses. The Operations Improvement Task Force, or OIT, was a review from the outside of how the state runs inside. And since the effort was a collaboration in the best spirit of that word, it's perhaps fitting that the F for Force fell off the abbreviation. QStP (pronounced Q-step) is the shorthand for Quality Services through Partnership. The word *step* is more than a chance acronym, though, for the process was a series of steps to build collaboration between labor and management inside state government in order to install continuous improvement both as a means and an end.

In his first State of the State Address, Governor Voinovich vowed that "hundreds of volunteer experts will look into every nook and cranny of state government" in a giant management audit of the state's operations. The approach had worked in Cleveland. "The task force created an entirely new attitude among our workers—someone listened and carried through on their recommendations," the governor said as he announced a similar review at the state level.

Auditors or reviewers—whatever one calls the people who did the work—were employed outside state government. The germane fact is that all were doing the OIT work as volunteers, neither expecting nor receiving money in return for their hours. A few key numbers underscore the magnitude of their contribution: more than 300 people donated more than 150,000 hours to the effort. They met, they probed, they reported. The result was nearly 1,600 recommendations for ways to save money, to withstand budget cuts without sacrificing quality, to eliminate duplication and waste. If the state had paid for their time and support services, it is estimated that the tab would have run to $14 million, which is enough cash to operate the average district school system for one year.

Organizing the volunteers took some management skill in and of itself. Heading the task was Robert Van Auken, former Cleveland banker. Volunteers served in one of five structures:

1. The Leadership Panel, consisting of forty Ohio business and industry leaders, supplied oversight and core support. Leadership Panelists came from Ohio's largest corporations and institutions, such as Bank One, Dayton Power & Light, Goodyear, Nationwide Insurance, and Ohio State University.

2. The Project Managers were representatives of two public accounting firms, Deloitte & Touche and Coopers & Lybrand. Their task was to advise teams on review methods and to ensure the validity of results.

3. The Agency Group Leaders were seven executives from OIT

sponsoring companies who each oversaw six to eight specialized teams that investigated related functions, a sort of middle
management. For example, one team might review all the state's
activities related to health inspections.

4. The Task Force Leaders, thirty-five executives, supervised daily
   activities of Task Force Team Members. It was these thirty-five
   who were responsible for reporting results.

5. Last were Task Force Members, nearly two hundred volunteers
   from sponsoring companies who collected and analyzed information in every state agency. That information included facts,
   recommendations, and opinions from state employees, from
   chairs of corresponding legislative committees, and from employees of each agency. To make the range of input even
   broader, reports included comments from people who wrote or
   phoned in ideas.

Most of the agency reviews were conducted between March and
September 1991, though some weren't finished until 1993. The OIT's
work did not end with the review process, however. Key volunteers
returned to their OIT posts to monitor progress on recommendations. At six-month intervals, they confirmed which recommendations had been completed correctly, which efforts needed correcting,
and which were on track toward completion.

Governor Voinovich remained personally involved throughout
the implementation phase of OIT. He pressured agency directors to
implement the recommendations or justify their noncompliance, according to one report prepared by the Office of Budget and Management. Progress made toward implementing recommendations
appeared on performance reviews of agency directors. By 1995 the
governor had called the entire process "the largest
private sector commitment to reinventing state gov-   *"Reinventing*
ernment anywhere in the country." Included in OIT   *state govern-*
were audits of the State Board of Education, Board   *ment"*
of Regents, all state universities, and the Bureau of
Workers' Compensation, as well as other cabinet-level state agencies.

Because so much effort went into drafting sound recommendations, it seems worthwhile to examine some of them here. Eleven recommendations were called "global issues" because they were beyond the purview of any one agency and affected several areas of state government. The first and foremost is value *per se*, what Governor Voinovich stressed in his 1992 State of the State Address as "a quality product for the least amount of money." Noting that state operations lacked performance measures, had poor communication and cooperation among agencies, and had lost focus on the customer, OIT reviewers did more than pronounce a need for improvement. In fact, the entire second phase of reinventing Ohio government, QStP, spun off from the recommendation that called for actions to engender quality. Specifics of global recommendation #1 read: (a) to create a focus on internal and external customers; (b) to establish an environment which facilitates team building, employee contribution and responsibility, risk taking, and innovation; (c) to analyze work processes and systems; and (d) to institutionalize a goal of continuous improvement. In short, the OIT urged the state of Ohio to adopt the concept of Total Quality Management.

Other global improvements called for were as follows: (2) training for top-level and middle-level managers, (3) revamping personnel policies, (4) reviewing programs within a framework of measurable outcomes, and (5) lobbying the legislature to revamp the Controlling Board, which is primarily a legislative committee but is staffed by the Office of Management and Budget. The board acts principally as the gatekeeper of budget flexibility and as the entity that waives competitive bidding. Established in 1917, the Controlling Board was thwarting its original role by micro-managing minute movements of dollars by 1991.

Global recommendation #6 dealt with asking for and getting federal dollars. Though the governor's Washington Office pursues federal money down several avenues, similar efforts from Columbus could be enhanced by staffing state agencies with people who have federal grant know-how, the OIT recommendation stated.

Centralizing debt management (global recommendation #7) was the OIT's response to Ohio's fragmented system of issuing debt. The final report suggested (a) establishing a three-tiered debt classification system of direct debt, revenue debt, and conduit debt; (b) managing direct debt to achieve specific ratios, with less than 5 percent of the General Revenue Fund devoted to debt service; (c) using accepted debt management practices and policies; (d) amending the Ohio Constitution to authorize an extended use of general obligation bonds; and (e) creating a central debt management staff.

OIT volunteers found a hodgepodge of energy practices. Their eighth global recommendation called for a state energy coordinator to work with agencies on adopting energy conservation practices. Similarly, the state began the conversion process to energy-efficient lighting, following the prescriptions of the federal Environmental Protection Agency. More significantly, the OIT document called for natural gas purchases on the open market, where shopping around might produce bulk purchase discounts.

Global recommendation #9 called for decentralization, particularly if moves could be made to economically depressed areas of Ohio. In its reproof for the state's lack of compliance with this recommendation, the OIT admitted that moving is expensive. Nonetheless, the state was commended for at least being on the lookout. The tenth OIT global recommendation aimed to enhance fund performance in the five retirement systems in Ohio. A Retirement Study Commission took on that task.

The last, and most sweeping, of the global recommendations dealt with duplication of effort, both administrative and programmatic. Noting that lack of coordination among agencies contributes not only to duplication but sometimes to antithetical efforts, the OIT proposed a grouping of agencies into functional units, thereby changing the governance structure. After study and consideration, the administration chose not to pursue this recommendation. Instead, related agencies were clustered for administrative purposes under Governor's Office executive assistants who reported directly to the governor.

Governor Voinovich had voiced his concern about the proliferation of boards and commissions that generated much of the duplication. In his 1991 State of the State Address, two years before the OIT report appeared, he cited the following statistics: "During the 1980s, state government created new boards and commissions to deal with just about every concern that came down the pike. There were 140 of them in 1980. Today, there are more than 235." He vowed "that the sun will set on some of them." As the OIT report hinted, that's a tall order when the prunees are agencies, boards, and commissions with varying degrees of independence and various allegiances. Nonetheless, by the 1997 State of the State Address, Governor Voinovich could say, "We have eliminated 121 boards and commissions." The self-described old gardener had once ruminated, "I have found over the years it takes a little pruning to have a healthy plant."

"It takes a little pruning to have a healthy plant."

Progress has been made on implementing OIT recommendations. According to data from the Governor's Office, about 90 percent of the administrative recommendations, 84 percent of the recommendations requiring legislation, and 85 percent of the executive recommendations had been implemented by the summer of 1998. Twelve state agencies had completed all of their OIT recommendations. Three-fourths of the remaining agencies had completed at least 80 percent of their recommendations. (Note: There were about 1,600 specific suggestions.) Monitoring the progress took the form of computerized tracking, complete with monthly scorecards that revealed exactly how an agency was advancing toward implementation completion.

What was not in the monitoring system, however, was a dollar total of savings achieved. Because few participants had control over the whole spending pie, it became impossible to state with accuracy how many dollars were saved by implementing specific recommendations in each slice. Yet the OIT report did venture to predict that $430 million would be saved if all the recommendations were implemented, a figure separate and apart from the value of the volunteers' gifts of time and money. Perhaps it would be instructive to look at a couple of specific recommendations, just to see how the process saved money, before reminding the reader to look for evidence of the spirit of the global recommendations incorporated in each agency's individual reports. In the Department of Administrative Services (DAS), adopting a "stockless supply" program for office supplies, paper, printer toner and the like reduced costs by $791,000, according to DAS estimates. Also in DAS, union and management developed a managed health care network that saved the state nearly $35 million in its first year.

Though saving taxpayer money is reward in itself, the OIT did design awards—one for cabinet directors, one for agencies, and one for individuals—who met certain compliance goals. And just to get the word out beyond the computerese of the tracking system, OIT published ten issues of a newsletter, *Ohio's Best*, so that everyone could read about the OIT revolution. Rewards were also earned by teams of employees who submitted money-saving ideas through the Innovation Ohio program, explained later in this chapter.

QUALITY SERVICES THROUGH PARTNERSHIP, OR QSTP

Think of QStP as the state of Ohio brand of Total Quality Management, a concept born in the 1950s and rejuvenated in the 1980s to describe best business practices. Built on the scholarship of W. Edward Deming, and expanded by Joseph Juran and Kaoru Ishikawa, the total quality concept puts the customer—in this case, the user of state services—center stage as the beneficiary of the state's efforts. Better serving this customer requires data-based decisions, teamwork among all the players, employee input, analysis of work processes, and a commitment to continuous improvement. But merely reciting a litany of management variables hardly tells the story of the Ohio campaign to initiate behavioral and cultural changes in its workplace. A quote from Governor Voinovich's first Inaugural Address reveals his view on the need for a system overhaul: "From this day forward, my goal as governor will be to reinstill in every state employee a sense of the tremendous opportunity we have before us to serve our fellow Ohioans and to make a difference in their lives. If we're going to get Ohio working up to its capacity again, then *we* must work up to *ours*."

> *"My goal as governor will be to reinstill in every state employee a sense of the tremendous opportunity we have before us to serve our fellow Ohioans and to make a difference in their lives."*

The foundation had been laid by OIT in its first global recommendation. Two responses in late 1991 then became steps one and two in QStP: (1) The Ohio Civil Service Employees Association (OCSEA) included key language in its bargaining agreement regarding joint actions to improve quality. (2) Governor Voinovich contacted David Kearns, chief executive officer of the Xerox Corporation, a company whose total quality management effort had succeeded demonstrably. The union was listening and a mentor was contacted for advice. Before the year was over, Xerox had upgraded its advice to support. Lent to guide Ohio into quality management was Xerox executive Jack Kindler.

In January 1992 Governor Voinovich took step three and invited Xerox executives to his cabinet retreat to explain the mechanics of quality management. According to the Quality Office's own account, seven agencies then agreed to experiment with the process. The pioneering seven were the Adjutant General's Office, Administrative Services, Development, Education, Mental Health, Transportation, and Youth Services. To those seven agency directors were added the executive director and presidents of five labor unions, the director of quality, and the director of cabinet affairs to form the Quality Steering Committee. It was time for school, step five. In April that year all the members of the Steering Committee underwent three and a half days of training. They in turn would become trainers of future students of quality. Their first assignment that April was a vision statement, their second was a term paper—a quality implementation plan. After advanced study at Xerox headquarters in Connecticut that November, the graduates were ready.

In January 1993 all the executive agencies designated quality coordinators and union liaisons, all of whom assembled with the Quality Steering Committee to hear the plans for implementation. Still, the massive undertaking needed fine-tuning. The February classes at Xerox headquarters this time focused on management/union relations. Signs that a partnership could form emerged on the plane ride home when the participants decided to rename Ohio's quality initiative Quality Services through Partnership. It was approximately step ten, but a significant one, because pivotal actions followed the rewording. The next step was to reconstitute the Steering Committee with equal numbers from union and management. Then the legislature acted. Passage of a bill funding a Quality Office made Ohio the first state in the nation to elevate quality to such prominence. A director was hired. QStP was finally off and running, catching up with Governor Voinovich's pledge in the 1993 State of the State Address: "Our goal is to change the culture of Ohio's workforce, to get every state employee excited about their jobs, and bring a new can-do spirit and enthusiasm into every state workplace."

Events in 1994 refined the training and sealed the bonds of partnership between union and management. Governor Voinovich also attended, with the presidents of Ohio's employee unions, the three-day updated training that all state employees ultimately would attend. As more and more state employees went through the QStP training and more and more teams formed, more and more improvements occurred and more and more success stories were shared. Governor Voinovich's second Inaugural Address in January 1995 was unequivocal about QStP's future: "Quality Services through Partnership will remain our number one management initiative in my second term. I am grateful to our unions for their ongoing partnership."

By 1995 bona fide praise emerged in the form of imitation. Officials from other states visited Ohio to learn about QStP. Ohio officials, in turn, visited other states to explain QStP. And Ohio quality teams were invited to demonstrate process improvements at various conferences. That was also the year that two how-to books by Ohio's Quality Office were distributed and widely read in state offices. The titles were *Guide for Creating a Process Improvement Team* and *Tool Kit for Quality*. State employees were no doubt gearing up for the first Team Up Ohio event, a type of fair with booths where teams actually demonstrated their process improvements. Total attendance was 650 for this milestone in the workplace revival. By the 1998 Team Up Ohio, attendance had risen to 4,000 state employees. One other high point of the quality story in 1995 was the commencement of the Quality Academy, a management school of sorts with beginning and advanced courses in such subjects as running an effective meeting, breakthrough creative thinking, and measurement basics for aspiring change agents. Advanced courses were added in 1996.

Five years after Governor Voinovich first conferred with Xerox management, QStP had reached a benchmark: every executive agency had a quality improvement team in place. It was therefore appropriate in 1996 to publish a recap of achievements in quality management. The first *Results Book* recounted dollar savings, error reductions, delay eradications, and customer satisfaction measures logged by several teams. Governor Voinovich not only read it, but he also encouraged his cabinet directors to aim to have at least one team story from their agencies in the next *Results Book*. Later that year Ohio hosted the All States Quality Forum, attended by people from twenty-one states, who stayed in Columbus an additional day to witness the second Team Up Ohio fair.

The QStP story then becomes one of bigger and better. Laudatory comments appeared in various publications, none more succinct than the March 9, 1997 *Washington Post:* "Ohio is one of the best examples of labor-management partnerships in government." Some summary data from the Quality Office will underscore its diffusion from a meeting between a governor and a business executive to an integral way to conduct state business. More than 50,000 state employees (about 88 percent of the total number of state employees) have completed the basic three-day training, which covers the problem-solving process, basic tools, and teamwork skills. That's enough people to equal a mid-sized city in Ohio, like Mansfield or Middletown. An additional 1,800 have completed advanced training to become facilitators, or guides, of the more than 2,500 process improvement teams. Though it's difficult to operationalize and measure such constructs as "customer satisfaction," one standard is eminently countable—dollars. The Quality Office has documented $75 million in savings, derived from doing things differently since 1993; and the quality documents qualify that number as a conservative estimate.

At the heart of the QStP movement, of course, is commitment to continuous improvement, which makes it a never-ending story in the effort to make "working harder and smarter" an institution in Ohio government. Governor Voinovich, too, continues to champion the effort. In his last State of the State Address in February 1998 he said, "Two weeks ago, 1,300 government managers and union leaders met to reaffirm their support for this program into the twenty-first century. With their continued partnership, I'm confident that Ohio will have America's first high-performance state government workforce."

"Ohio will have America's first high-performance state government workforce."

QUALITY FINANCIAL MANAGEMENT

While OIT and QStP both focus on the activities of people doing their jobs, one goal of those activities is to do the job more efficiently, whether by individuals or teams. Cost cutting in the workplace is a necessary, but not sufficient, condition for restoring a state's financial health. Governor Voinovich's Office of Budget and Management (OBM) has identified achievements that contributed to a second-tier money-saver in the state's operations—a lower bond rating, which means paying interest at a lower rate to borrow money. These achievements fall into three categories: (1) What OBM termed Governor Voinovich's "aggressive conservatism with regard to state spending" accounts for part of the improved financial health. (2) Changes in tax policy to enhance business expansion in Ohio or business relocation to Ohio—as well as tax cuts for Ohioans—explain some of the improvement. (3) Plain old-fashioned savings, more money in the Rainy Day Fund, tell part of the story, along with a new savings account called the Human Services Stabilization Fund.

Spending Less

When George Voinovich took the oath of office as governor in 1991, Ohio was in financial straits that the word *crisis* understates. As he said in the 1991 State of the State Address, "It is safe to say that we have never before found ourselves in the midst of a financial crisis of the magnitude we face today." When he settled into his chair in the Governor's Office, George Voinovich faced a projected budget shortfall of a billion and a half dollars. (The very chair itself became a symbol of the frugality the dire situation called for. Rather than permit the state to spend $1,300 on a new chair, Governor Voinovich brought his old favorite from Cleveland.) Calling for a close scrutiny of the way Ohio spent taxpayer dollars, the governor posited, "Gone are the days when public officials are measured by how much they spend on a problem," which was the prelude to his hallmark credo:

"We must work harder and smarter, and do more with less."

"We must work harder and smarter, and do more with less." It is one of the governor's best-known quotes and was cited in the 1992 book *Reinventing Government: How the Entrepreneurial Spirit Is Transforming the Public Sector* by David Osborne and Ted Gaebler.

It was a given in the years preceding Voinovich's tenure as governor that the state budget grew every year. In his first year in office, Governor Voinovich broke that pattern. For fiscal year 1992 he proposed to spend fewer dollars than the previous year's budget had allowed. And he kept the brakes on. The four budgets written during his eight years in office represent the lowest rate of growth in state spending in thirty years. Of course the economy improved during those eight years, but one set of figures shows that state spending didn't accelerate when the economy did. From 1991 to 1996, total Ohio personal income grew by 28.56 percent while the state's General Revenue Fund (GRF) spending grew by 26.85 percent, according to OBM data. In the preceding decade, growth in state spending had always exceeded personal income growth.

One ax at Governor Voinovich's disposal for exercising aggressive conservatism was the executive order. In his first three years in office, he issued four separate orders for budget cuts that the OBM credits with saving the state $711 million. Equally significant was the phenomenon of underspending. In the three years 1995–98, General Revenue Fund spending was below budgeted levels by a total of more than $2.7 billion. The OBM pointed to a robust economy as one key explanation for the GRF savings and underspending on Medicaid as another. Elimination of General Assistance for able-bodied people spared dollars in the budget, while spending below budgeted figures showed up in Aid to Dependent Children and other welfare programs. While programs for families, children, and the aged were not immune to the budget knife, amounts set for those particular programs had been designed to avoid cutbacks in service to people most at risk. As the governor said in the 1992 State of the State Address, "We chose to target our scarce resources on people, and particularly those most at risk—women, children, and senior citizens." The surpluses, though an immediate advantage in budget balancing, proved to have long-term benefits as well, as the following section on the Rainy Day Fund explains.

Reductions in spending were not enough, however, in 1992. As Ohio's budget woes continued, it became apparent that more revenue was necessary to stabilize the FY 1993 budget in order to avoid what the administration called "destructive cuts" and to head off future tax increases. Consequently, in 1992 a tax package was passed in a bipartisan budget balancing act that tapped more than a dozen sources of revenue in order to close the $200 million gap that remained that fiscal year. On an annualized basis the changes (some of which have since been repealed) generated about $400 million in new revenue.

The changes in tax policy under Governor Voinovich are so numerous and cross so many agency lines that they are detailed elsewhere in this volume. For example, changes in the corporate franchise tax are discussed in Chapter 3, "Jobs and Economic Development," because that change was aimed at attracting new or expanded business to Ohio. Likewise, personal income tax exemptions and rate reductions constitute a form of economic development for individual households and are therefore taken up in Chapter 3. To sum up, tax cuts were a major tactic in the campaign to improve the business climate in Ohio and hence the state's financial ratings. Suffice it to say here that massive tax restructuring was among the prescriptions that improved Ohio's financial position.

Saving More

The third stratagem used to manage finances better was to increase the dollars in the state's Budget Stabilization Fund, a formal name rarely heard in public. Referred to instead as the Rainy Day Fund, it is essentially a savings account, a contingency for those economic downturns beyond the control of even the best money managers. Economic recessions can force two reactions by a state that are anathema to everybody—budget cuts and tax increases. Savings can head off either of those two eventualities. Yet the recession that met George Voinovich at the Governor's Office door forced a depletion of the Rainy Day Fund in order to keep the budget balanced. It was 1993 before economic improvements and good management permitted deposits into the nearly empty savings fund, which sank to 14¢ at its lowest point. Deposits have been made every year since. The surpluses from the 1995–98 budgets also fed the fund. By the end of 1998, the Rainy Day Fund balance was $906.9 million, or 5 percent of fiscal year 1998 revenues, according to OBM reports. The governor and legislature also created a separate savings account for human services. More than a mere buffer in times of recession, the new fund positioned Ohio to deal with the coming decentralization of human services programs from Washington.

Rating Debtworthiness

While Governor Voinovich's financial management efforts can be measured with a variety of yardsticks, one of the most significant—in terms of the state's continued financial improvement—is recognition in the form of the state's bond rating, which reflects a state's capacity to manage its finances. Ohio's General Obligation (GO) bond rating had not budged since it had been downgraded during the recession of 1979. But in 1996, two premier bond rating agencies gave Ohio improved marks. Standard and Poor's increased Ohio's GO rating from AA to AA+, and Moody's Investors Service raised its rating from Aa to Aa1. Those grades mean more than praise. According to OBM figures, the state would save about $4 million each year on borrowing costs for the life of a typical year's worth of bonds issued by the state (about $900 million). Among the ten states with the largest populations, Ohio was tied with New Jersey for the highest bond rating in late 1996. Among all debt-issuing states, Ohio ranked tenth, according to the OBM.

Other sources outside state government, and thus considered more objective, gave Ohio high marks for financial management. Fitch Investors Service rated Ohio's GO debt at AA+. *Financial World* magazine moved Ohio from thirty-first among states in its 1993 rankings to twelfth in its 1995 rankings in the financial management category. Aside from the financial gurus, *Governing* magazine also recognized Ohio's financial achievements in honoring Governor Voinovich as "Public Official of the Year" in 1995, based in large part on his prudent money management. "Voinovich applied the same formula to pulling Cleveland out of its crisis as he has to running

Ohio: Put together a top administrative team to run your government and forge public-private economic development partnerships to build your economy," wrote the editors of *Governing*. When he recited these financial achievements in his 1997 State of the State Address, Governor Voinovich had a terser explanation: "First and foremost, we have been fiscally conservative."

"First and foremost, we have been fiscally conservative."

Doing More with Nothing

If the extent of Governor Voinovich's conservatism had ended at the state line, it would be explanation enough for the brighter prospects in Ohio. But he took the ethic of working harder and smarter to Washington as well, where members of Congress had been promulgating a prescription of doing more with a whole lot less—nothing. Known as unfunded mandates, these federal laws dictate dos and don'ts but provide no wherewithal to achieve them. Governor Voinovich fought for release from what he called Washington's "activism on the cheap." In 1993, two years after his first inauguration, his Washington Office had completed a study titled *The Need for a New Federalism: Federal Mandates and Their Impact on the State of Ohio*, which became a resource in the ensuing lobbying effort to effect Congressional change. Governor Voinovich mobilized a coalition of state and local government organizations to work with House and Senate leaders in drafting the Unfunded Mandate Reform Act, which passed in 1995. Though existing mandates were not removed, relief came in the act's proscriptions regarding future mandates. One provision, the point-of-order procedure, gives any House or Senate member the authority to question an unfunded mandate. Although a question does not equal a veto, the point-of-order may explain why more potential mandates now founder in committees or are withdrawn altogether. What can be safely concluded is that fewer unfunded mandates translate into Ohio dollars freed up for other purposes, a figure as hard to estimate as its existence is easy to establish. The governor himself estimated that local governments in Ohio spent twelve cents of every dollar on un-funded mandates in 1994.

The major achievements in the category of management detailed so far had ramifications in nearly every state agency. In addition, the spirit of "work harder and smarter, do more with less" manifested it-self in agency-specific ways. The following review of the less publi-cized achievements in management during Governor Voinovich's eight years in Columbus is arranged by state agency in alphabetical order. Derivation from OIT, QStP, or fiscal conservatism is not the sole set of reasons for their inclusion. Whatever is new with far-reaching impact that fits the rubric of "reinventing government" is included.

ADMINISTRATIVE SERVICES

The mission statement of the Department of Administrative Services (DAS) reads like this: "Providing quality service to our customers in order to lead, support, and facilitate the efficient operation of gov-ernment." As the engine room of Governor Voinovich's ship of state, the Administrative Services department took on a heavy load in im-plementing quality procedures in state government. What the unit it-self calls DAS 2000 is the label for an overhaul of DAS organization and procedures to meet new challenges. It took an act of the 121st General Assembly to execute some of the DAS 2000 changes in pur-chasing procedures, the civil service system and the capital improve-ments process. The most visible change was in departmental organization, with a blending of six divisions into four: General Ser-vices, Computer Services, Human Resources, and Equal Opportu-nity. Doing more with less also resulted in a reduction in the number and complexity of administrative rules. The sheer number of rules in DAS was reduced by 58 percent, with parings in two specific areas as follows: purchasing laws were reduced from 34 to 11, while construc-tion compliance and affirmative action rules were downsized from 25 to 14. The department's documents also describe the new rules as "user friendly," reflecting a further effort to reduce what the private sector would call bureaucracy.

Governor Voinovich was directly involved in at least three of the numerous specific changes in DAS. The first was a call to study the management of the state's information technology apparatus. Recommendations were made by the Information Management Reengineering Project in 1996 to overlay some structure onto the content the computer revolution had wrought in state office buildings. The next year, on the recommendation of the Project, Governor Voinovich issued an executive order to create the Interagency Information Management Group (IMG) of cabinet members, chaired by the Chief Information Officer. Their goal is to ensure consistency in technological decision making.

DAS was also the force behind a switch from an aging microwave system to a new network that serves all the state's telecommunications needs. With a name so intricate that it goes by the acronym SONET, the new infrastructure handles telephone usage; voice, video, and data transmission; and computer linkage at reduced trunk-line cost. Begun in 1991, the digital fiber optic hydra serves 54 public radio and television stations, 250 public libraries, 3,600 public schools, 100 colleges and universities, 100 state agencies, health and safety communications, state telephones, and the state lottery. The initiatives discussed in later chapters, such as SchoolNet and the library network OPLIN, would not have been possible without SONET.

A second initiative in DAS with Governor Voinovich's imprimatur is titled Ohio Geographically Referenced Information Program (OGRIP), which permits the sharing of digitally mapped data among several entities in both the public and private sectors. State agencies, universities, local government units, public utilities, private businesses, and individuals who access geographic information had shared data informally as early as 1989, but their efforts won official sanction in a 1993 executive order by Governor Voinovich that gave OGRIP an operating budget and a state office. Just as wire services cut costs for news organizations that adopted the telegraph 150 years ago, consortiums like OGRIP let participants pool and share infor-mation that is costly to digitize. Word of OGRIP has spread to other states, which seek to duplicate this Ohio model for technological co-operation between the public and private sectors.

A third function that Governor Voinovich was involved in within DAS is the Historically Underutilized Business Program (HUB). Established in 1997 by executive order, the HUB program certifies businesses owned by socially and economically disadvantaged indi-viduals. The order also set a goal: all cabinet agencies should try to spend 5 percent of available contracting dollars in construction as well as supplies and services with HUBs. Other innovations for HUBs at the DAS division of Equal Opportunity include a dual cer-tification program with the Department of Transportation and assis-tance in registering with the Office of State Purchasing for future bidding opportunities. DAS reported in 1998 that more than 180 companies had been certified as HUBs.

Administrative Services' list of changes to improve efficiency in-cludes six other innovations in the management category.

1. The traditional employee suggestion award program, which had begun in 1972, evolved under a DAS program called Inno-vation Ohio, which aimed to encourage the contribution of ideas by teams, in the QStP mode. Since Innovation Ohio began in 1994, employee suggestions have saved the state more than $16 million.

2. Shopping for the best deals in managed health care will be discussed as a cost-cutting tool elsewhere, but it would be an oversight not to mention here that DAS developed and imple-mented the managed care plan for Ohio's 60,000 employees. Named Ohio Med, the plan is consistently cheaper than tradi-tional fee-for-service plans. Ohio was one of the early adopters of managed care for its employees. Initial savings for the state were $34.9 million in its first year (1992), according to DAS figures. Savings in subsequent years have averaged about $823,000 per year.

3. With the wonder of computers, DAS can now post payroll information electronically instead of on paper. The Paperless Payroll that zips along to 240 payroll offices in the state saves time and money—$823,000 annually.

4. The state printing functions, housed in DAS, also saw improvements during the last eight years. Beginning in 1996, printing contracts were awarded through a competitive sealed bid process. And the state's In-House Publishing Center moved into a renovated facility that permits improved services.

5. Taking the cue from OIT's global recommendation to develop an energy policy, the DAS Office of Energy Services was created in 1994. It directs energy economizing on several fronts, from scrutinizing utility rates, to buying natural gas at discounts, even to monitoring renovations and new construction for wise choices in design and equipment. The office has reported its savings at $7 million across eight years.

6. Another new use of technology that has saved time and trees is the Fax Back system in DAS's Office of State Purchasing. Vendors interested in learning about the state's advertised bids can phone Fax Back, respond to prompts on the menu of options, and receive information via automatic fax. Begun only a year before this writing, the system has logged more than 4,700 calls.

DAS is also charged with various education functions, one of which is training "customers" how to do business with the state. Since that instruction remains strictly within the focus of running the state, it is mentioned here rather than in the broader education category of Chapter 4. The customers, or students, are state employees, vendors doing business with Ohio, and construction businesses. A sampling of the courses offered includes civil service law, human resources procedures, mechanics of purchasing, doing business with the state, and the competitive sealed bid process.

Administrative Services also conducts conferences, some in conjunction with other agencies. Ten of these efforts will be described, for they serve large numbers of people who are essentially partners in managing the state's functions. The conference with the highest enrollment is the Intergovernmental Technology Conference (ITC), begun in 1993. More than 15,000 people attended the 1998 conference, making the ITC the largest government technology conference in the Midwest. In 1998 employees from federal, state, and local governments from fifty states and six foreign nations converged on Columbus to learn the latest in governmental uses of technology. Also begun in 1993 were the Human Resources Conferences (HRC). Human resources administrators, payroll officers, equal employment opportunity officers, and labor relations specialists attend the twice-annual HRCs to stay current on such topics as legislative changes that affect their bailiwicks and how diversity should be handled in the workplace. The 1998 Human Resources Conference attracted eight hundred participants. A separate conference is conducted for human resources officials at the county level. Held annually since 1995, the county-level version focuses on such issues as recruitment strategies, early retirement incentive programs, and guidelines for presenting a case before the State Personnel Board of Review.

Companies wishing to do business with the state of Ohio can choose from different types of DAS conferences. The oldest of these is the Ohio Business Expo, begun in 1993 because Governor Voinovich wanted Ohio vendors and government purchasing agents to meet and to exchange information—a sort of marketplace for buying and selling supplies and services needed to run a state. Cohosted with the departments of Agriculture, Development, and Natural Resources, the Expo was first called the Buy Ohio Conference, a name that underscores the principle that only Ohio-based businesses need apply to the annual event in Columbus. Narrower in scope was the series of conferences called Doing Business with the State of Ohio in the 21st Century. The name may be long, but it captures the essence of the 1997–98 conferences held in Akron, Toledo, Cincinnati, and Columbus. Explaining the variety of business opportunities available through state government and promoting the use of new technology to conduct that business were the twin emphases of the Doing Business conferences, which were attended by 675 vendors. The Department of Development lent a hand with its breakout sessions on what the state does to boost business creation and growth. The Office of the State Architect in the DAS General Services Division handled two rounds of seminars in 1996 to aid those involved in capital construction projects. Round one, Critical Path Method, tackled the complexities of scheduling and sequencing construction projects. Round two, How to Do Business with the Office of the State Architect, enjoys a self-explanatory title, but those seminars also unveiled new and improved contracts and documents required for state construction projects.

Three conferences focused on increasing the minority presence in state business. The first Minority Business Partnership Symposium, cosponsored by the Department of Rehabilitation and Correction in 1996, brought more than 425 representatives of Minority Business Enterprises (MBEs) together with state purchasing experts to explore business opportunities. One conference, called the Minority Business Update, was convened to explain Governor Voinovich's 1997 HUB executive order. More than 200 minority businesses sent representatives to hear those details. In order to increase the numbers of certified minority MBEs and HUBs that bid on state contracts, DAS and the Department of Development teamed up in 1998 to provide training sessions at Minority Contractors Business Assistance Program offices throughout Ohio.

One improvement to managing information has only recently moved past the planning stage. The Multi-Agency Radio Communications System (MARCS), a DAS responsibility, will replace a current radio communication system that is sixty years old. MARCS is designed to provide instant voice and data communications statewide for public safety and emergency management services in a single system shared by twelve state agencies.

A thorough review of Administrative Services accomplishments since 1991 must include the DAS administration of various capital projects beyond the formalities of advertising bids and signing contracts. Foremost among these is the first restoration of the Ohio Statehouse since its completion 137 years ago. The elegance of 1860s décor in 1990s materials masks the wiring and cabling for twenty-first-century technology, all of which is protected by a state-of-the-art sprinkler system. DAS data for the first two years since the grand reopening in 1996 count 350,000 visitors to the centerpiece of Capitol Square. Dedicated on the Statehouse grounds in 1998 was Veterans' Plaza, the state's first memorial to honor those who served in World War II, Korea, Vietnam, and the Gulf War. An accounting of the Statehouse renovation would be incomplete without mentioning that the inscription "With God, all things are possible" was cast in bronze and inlaid in the sidewalk leading to the main Statehouse door. Aides tell the story about how the governor got the idea for displaying the state seal and motto while on a trade mission in India. When an inscription on a public building caught his eye, he stopped to look at it and remarked that a similar bronze casting would be appropriate in Columbus.

Another major construction project overseen by the State Architect's Office in DAS was the Hilltop project. Formally opened in April 1998, the two office buildings on Broad Street in Columbus that now house the departments of Public Safety and Transportation provide workspace for more than 2,000 employees, who can walk from one building to the other via an underground tunnel. Not only was the project completed on time, it was also $14 million under budget. Of the contracts associated with the Hilltop construction, Ohio-based companies got 87 percent, while minority businesses got 22.6 percent.

Other construction projects that stand as showplaces of Ohio's eminence are the two Centers of Science and Industry (COSI). DAS oversaw the completion of the new COSI in Toledo and the beginning of the replacement COSI in Columbus. Though some business people view the COSIs through the lens of economic development, thousands of Ohio schoolchildren see them as, well, lots of fun.

DEPARTMENT OF AGRICULTURE

Creation of a stand-alone Division of Dairy within the Department of Agriculture was another example of OIT at work. Prior to the passage in 1997 of the Dairy Modernization Act (which the Agriculture Department strongly supported), responsibility for Grade A milk inspection was divided between two divisions within the department. In what may be one of the least debatable management improvements ordained by OIT, the act creating the dairy division was supported by the dairy industry and was approved by the General Assembly unanimously.

Another effort to eliminate duplication took form in the Food Safety Council, a study group that worked to modernize and standardize Ohio's regulations for food retailers and restaurants. The public-private council consisted of members from the food industry as well as from affected state agencies. Licensing and inspections had been scattered among units not only in Agriculture, but also in the Department of Health and in local health departments. In May 1998 the council made recommendations to the General Assembly for uniform food safety standards and for the elimination of duplication in licensing and inspection.

In another reshuffling to put expertise where it is readily accessible, Governor Voinovich approved agricultural liaison positions at the departments of Environmental Protection and Development to improve both regulation of and assistance to the agricultural industry.

OFFICE OF BUDGET AND MANAGEMENT (OBM)

As the state's official accounting firm, OBM does more than fill in the numbers on ledger pages. During the Voinovich administration, OBM implemented its own operations improvements as well as helping to guide changes in other agencies. Within OBM itself, one improvement was gathering information for an inventory of all state programs. It had been noted that line items in an agency's budget did not necessarily paint an accurate picture of the programs and achievements of that agency, nor was it easy to compare the efforts of different agencies. To correct the problem, OBM completed a description of cabinet-level programs by 1994. Now in its third edition, the State Government Book is the repository of information on all programs conducted by all state agencies. OBM also edited its budget document to comply with the standards of the Government Finance Officers Association, an effort that resulted in Ohio's first Distinguished Budget Presentation Award from the national GFOA.

OBM even fulfills a journalistic role in its *Budget Highlights* documents, first published in 1993. Whereas earlier OBM briefing documents merely described the executive recommendations submitted to the General Assembly, *Budget Highlights* recaps the final product after enactment by the legislature. In addition to debits and credits, or state spending and revenues, the document headlines effects on policy reflected by the budget. Another significant improvement at OBM was an upgrade to the Central Accounting System to make it more user-friendly.

Because the Controlling Board functions within OBM jurisdiction, it fell to the agency to implement the OIT recommendation to streamline Controlling Board functions. OBM wrote yet another book, a procedures manual accompanied by automated forms, which introduced speed and consistency to the request process. Though OBM does not audit individual state agencies, it did devise a comprehensive program for internal controls that aids agencies in improving their own oversight efforts. OBM was also the agency that brought the electronic payment card to state government purchasing for small dollar amounts, which comprise almost 80 percent of the purchases logged by the Central Accounting System. In another challenge met by OBM during the Voinovich administration, the legislature charged OBM with the financial review phase of the Central State University rescue, a three-year team effort that untangled the record keeping of the school.

Last in an accounting of OBM's achievements is the agency's role in the major policy changes during the Voinovich years. More than the presenter of pertinent numbers, OBM lent expertise to the following policy initiatives: developing the *Ohio 2000/Ohio First* document, restructuring the Department of Commerce, reforming education finances, developing the School Facilities Commission, setting up computer and telecommunications learning networks, shaping Ohio Family and Children First, establishing the Office of Quality Services within its own ranks, and creating the Interagency Information Management Group.

DEPARTMENT OF COMMERCE

As one of the larger agencies of the executive branch, the Department of Commerce has more opportunities to work harder and smarter. Governor Voinovich played a major role in several changes in the management category within Commerce. One of the most extensive was an OIT-driven plan to restructure the department. In legislation called the Governor's Cabinet Restructuring Bill, Commerce absorbed new management duties. First, two cabinet-level agencies were eliminated. The Department of Industrial Relations became the *Division* of Industrial *Compliance* within Commerce. The Department of Liquor Control was split between two agencies: Commerce now oversees permitting and licensing, while Public Safety handles enforcement. Then three existing divisions within Commerce related to money and banking were distilled into a single unit titled the Division of Financial Institutions. The new configuration handles the chartering, regulation, and examination of banks, credit unions, savings and loans, savings banks, and consumer finance companies. The restructuring eliminated duplication, true, but also expanded the role of the Department of Commerce as one of Ohio's chief regulatory agencies. The new Division of Financial Institutions also assimilated the regulatory function of the former Division of Consumer

Finance, which was eliminated from division status at Commerce. The licensing functions of the defunct Division of Consumer Finance moved to the Division of Real Estate and Professional Licensing, which is yet another new label in the Department of Commerce overhaul.

There was a compelling reason to remove Liquor Control from the governor's cabinet. State liquor stores were privatized between 1991 and 1996, in a move that saved the state an estimated $24 million annually. The savings accrued from the elimination of store operating expenses such as leases, utilities, security, salaries, and benefits. Under the private system, the state still owns and controls spiritous liquor, but the private stores contract with the state to make the sales. By 1996 the number of liquor stores converted from public to private was 263. According to data from Commerce, profits from liquor sales in fiscal year 1997 were $115 million, of which $88 million poured into the General Revenue Fund. That's about a one-fifth increase in revenue over FY 1996, even though liquor sales have fallen since 1991.

Though various management changes between 1991 and 1998 were motivated by the working harder and smarter credo, the need to modernize explains a few modifications. One example is the recodification of the banking industry that the Department of Commerce secured with the passage of House Bill 538. It was the first time the issue had been revisited in thirty years. With the updating came a reduction in bureaucracy that fits the Voinovich fashion of streamlining.

A fourth initiative that the governor sought has economic development ramifications, but is discussed here because its hallmark is simplification of a management process. The consolidation of all approvals for construction plan review came under one roof—literally. With the creation of the Division of Industrial Compliance in the Commerce shakeup, it became possible for one unit to handle all the sign-offs related to construction. Prior to the creation of this one-stop shop, a builder had to process paperwork in three separate state agencies in three different locations. In the spring of 1997 the new customer service center began issuing permits, approving plans, and dispatching inspectors. Also melded into the code operations at the new Division of Industrial Compliance were plumbing regulations, which were moved from the aegis of the Department of Health.

Welding is probably not an activity most people consider when they think about reducing bureaucracy, but the governor saw an opportunity in that trade to establish order in what had been a somewhat chaotic certification process. In short, the new welder certification program lets pipe welders transfer their skills from one job to another without being retested and recertified every time they pack up their torches. The problem stemmed from the difficulty in writing uniform specifications for various welding procedures. A bureaucratic behemoth creaked along rather than addressing the tough writing assignments. The new training and certification program creates a pool of pretested welders available to contractors. What's more, this aspect of management improvement is administered and paid for by cosponsors—the United Association of Plumbers and Pipefitters and the Mechanical Contractors Association.

One of the nearly 1,600 specific recommendations of the Operations Improvement Task Force dealt with the issue of prevailing wage, or how much governments must pay outside workers for construction or improvements to public buildings and roads. Though the change was initiated by the industrial compliance unit of Commerce, setting the actual wage and enforcing compliance are managed by the Department of Employment Services. In short, the prevailing wage must be paid to workers when the cost of the job will exceed a certain predetermined amount, called a threshold. The prevailing wage itself is defined by rates from collective bargaining agreements specific to type of work and locality. The law signed by Governor Voinovich in March 1994 introduced five changes to a statute that had stood unaltered since 1976. (1) The threshold for new construction was increased from $4,000 to $50,000. (2) A new threshold category for repairs, alterations, and painting was set at $15,000. (3) Contracts with soil and water conservation districts and petitioned county ditch projects were exempted. (4) Penalties on intentional violators were payable to employees as well as to the Division of Industrial Compliance. (5) Suspensions of contractors who willfully violate the law were toughened. In later action, schools were exempted in 1997. The law was a money-saver. One study estimated the annual savings to state, city, and local governments at $6.8 million, given that prevailing wages add about 13 percent to construction costs.

Though countless unsung volunteers aided their fellow Ohioans during the disastrous flooding of 1997, Commerce got an official call from Governor Voinovich to use its personnel to staff the Emergency Operations Center in Columbus as well as six regional disaster recovery centers throughout Southern Ohio. Department of Commerce inspectors donated the time to complete more than 1,400 free inspections. Other employees supervised a 24-hour safety hotline, while those in the bedding inspection unit repaired and donated hundreds of blankets, comforters, and even toys for flood victims and their children.

Other management improvements in Commerce during the Voinovich years were creation of the Cemetery Commission to register cemeteries and handle complaints, expansion of outreach by the Division of Unclaimed Funds in order to get more money back to its rightful owners, and experimentation with regional customer service centers for construction permitting.

DEPARTMENT OF HUMAN SERVICES

Though Human Services was fully occupied implementing welfare reform, which in Ohio is an economic development matter, some of its achievements improved the delivery of longstanding services and thus fit in the management chapter. Chief of these is containing Medicaid costs. As Governor Voinovich said in the 1991 State of the State Address, "Medicaid costs in the Department of Human Services continue to soar, propelled by double-digit growth in long-term care costs, growth we must work together to bring under control." One cure was managed care, the 1990s solution to spiraling medical costs. The state's sheer size gives it the ability to leverage quality care at the lowest cost. Ohio's version of privatizing Medicaid, called OhioCare, was approved by the federal government in early 1995. The means for predicting costs and designating access used by health maintenance organizations was purchased for seventeen counties by 1997. Human Services now contracts with eleven HMOs to provide health care services to more than 249,000 welfare-related Medicaid recipients in Ohio. Because OhioCare did not pertain to nursing home reimbursements, a prospective reimbursement system was devised to help lower Ohio's Medicaid tab in that area. By 1996 Governor Voinovich could report savings figures to Ohioans in his State of the State Address. "We have done much to contain the Medicaid pacman, which grew by 245 percent in Ohio over the last ten years, a decade in which its share of the state budget soared from 19 to 30 percent." In fact, in fiscal 1997, Ohio's major Medicaid program decreased by 0.9 percent—the first decrease in expenditures since 1970. The caseload had dropped by 1998 to 1.1 million people at a cost estimated at $5.4 billion in FY 1999. Human Services staffers processed 55 billion separate claims for Medicaid services from more than 36,000 individual and institutional health care providers who billed the state in FY 1997.

A second money-saver in Human Services was its increased collection of child support. When child support is collected, the state is relieved of some of the cost of services like Temporary Assistance to Needy Families and food stamps. The figures for the years 1991–98 show an 81 percent increase in collections, to $1.5 billion. In addition to working harder and smarter, Human Services got a new tool when the 1995 welfare reform bill required employers to report newly hired people to Human Services so that the names could be cross-checked against the delinquent child-support list. Another method the state introduced to increase child support was designating three private collection agencies to track down delinquent payments. By 1998, seventy-four counties had used one of the three private agencies. Yet another get-tough approach was the state's suspension of the professional licenses of parents owing child support. Because collecting from fathers obviously cannot take place unless their names are known, a 1997 state law eased the process for voluntary acknowledgments of paternity while the mothers are in the hospital. Between 1991 and 1998 the number of established paternities more than doubled in Ohio. And the most novel tactic of all was the governor's "Most Wanted" posters featuring names and faces of the worst deadbeats. The various efforts won Ohio the Outstanding Program Achievement award from the National Child Support Enforcement Association in 1997.

Human Services put to work new technologies that helped manage three types of information about its clients. The Integrated Client Management System provides counties with a system for assessing and tracking services to families. The Statewide Child Welfare Information System does the same just for children. The Early Fraud Detection and Prevention Program catches ineligible recipients before applications are approved. Since the inception of computerized fraud detection in 1991, more than 90,000 referrals have been investigated and completed. The high mark in cost savings for one month that the detection system tallied was $10 million. All three are networked to other databases to speed and simplify the management of information.

DEPARTMENT OF INSURANCE

As in most of the agencies, many of the management successes in Insurance are tied to the use of technology. One achievement, however, is purely a measure of quality. The National Association of Insurance Commissioners conferred accreditation on Ohio's Department of Insurance in the area of financial solvency regulation. Various bills sponsored by Insurance and passed by the General

Assembly positioned the department to earn the regulatory accreditation, which was renewed in 1996.

Another key innovation in Insurance management was the 1997 passage of the Managed Care Uniform Licensure Act, which gave the department regulatory authority where none had existed before over new types of health insurance, such as preferred provider organizations (PPO), health maintenance organizations (HMO), and physician hospital organizations (PHO). Among the other changes in the Department of Insurance were new antifraud rules, which required insurers to put antifraud plans in writing and to report suspected fraud to the state, and new statutes shepherded through the General Assembly to reform various aspects of the insurance regulation function of the department. One in-house change was the creation of the Financial Surveillance Section, which monitors the solvency of insurance companies, within the Office of Financial Regulation Services. Like their colleagues in the Department of Commerce, employees of the Department of Insurance went to the aid of fellow Ohioans during four floods, assisting with insurance claims in the hardest hit counties and directing people without insurance to other services. Governor Voinovich commented on the aid people gave each other during the 1997 flood in his 1998 State of the State Address: "As devastating as that flood was, it also reminded us what it is to be an Ohioan. It reminded us of the strength, the resilience, and the willingness to help one's neighbor that surely enabled our earliest pioneers to survive in the wilderness that was Ohio. And it proved to us that those proud traits have worn well through the 195 years since statehood."

DEPARTMENT OF MENTAL HEALTH

Since 1990 the Department of Mental Health has overseen the closing of five state hospitals, the privatization of one, and the merging of six more into three—all in an effort to redirect mental health dollars and management to the local level. According to department records, more than $600 million has been redirected to locally managed mental health systems by these actions. Another result has been a reduction in staff-to-patient ratio in state facilities to the lowest level in seven years—1.97 to 1.

Evidence of OIT's global recommendation to group similar functions across agencies shows up in the consolidation of laboratory services between the departments of Mental Health and of Rehabilitation and Correction into a Unified Lab. A more recent attempt to combine efforts when agencies share outcome goals is the Interdepartmental Diversions Program. Initiated by Governor Voinovich, the experimental program focuses on assessment, intervention, and treatment for mentally ill and/or substance-abusing offenders before they move into the criminal justice system. Five state agencies and five counties plan and fund linkages in services to reach people who might not be served under existing management structures. The departments of Alcohol and Drug Addiction Services, Rehabilitation and Correction, and Youth Services and the Office of Criminal Justice Services join with Mental Health and the counties of Cuyahoga, Hamilton, Lorain, Summit, and Trumbull in the Interdepartmental Diversions projects. Early reports are optimistic, but the final evaluation of individuals served and the entities serving them won't be completed until January 1999.

DEPARTMENT OF MENTAL RETARDATION AND DEVELOPMENTAL DISABILITIES (MRDD)

In the 1993 State of the State Address, Governor Voinovich said one of his goals was "to replace our often fragmented social service delivery system with better coordinated local partnerships." He also emphasized on several occasions that residential care is preferable to institutional care for all ages. That philosophy figures prominently in the initiatives in Mental Retardation and Development Disabilities

(MRDD). Procedures were changed to permit Medicaid reimbursement for various services rendered in independent or residential settings. Furthermore, MRDD is the clearinghouse for allocating money to county MRDD boards for housing for people with developmental disabilities. Through the Capital Housing Program, county MRDD boards work in conjunction with local housing authorities or independently to acquire and manage living space such as single-family dwellings, duplexes, and condominiums.

Another thread in the fabric of noninstitutional services delivered locally is MRDD's increase in federal reimbursements through the Community Alternative Funding System (CAFS). The cost of medical and support services for persons with mental retardation and developmental disabilities is paid to county MRDD boards, schools, or nonprofit organizations. Though CAFS first appeared in 1989, reimbursements under its aegis totaled only $150,000 in its first year. The fiscal year 1998 total is more than $100 million. Because such an increase in money and administrative responsibility shifted to the counties, management shifted, too. The state now provides funds for county MRDD boards to hire business managers.

DEPARTMENT OF PUBLIC SAFETY

The most sweeping management change in Public Safety was the addition of several operations to the department's umbrella. The Emergency Management Agency, liquor enforcement, investigation of food stamp fraud, and Public Utilities Commission enforcement were transferred from other agencies in 1995. The Office of Emergency Medical Services was transferred to Public Safety in 1992. Another improvement in emergency preparedness came with the construction in 1994 of the Emergency Operations Center, which is shared with other state agencies. Still on the drawing board is the Incident Command System, another collaborative venture in the emergency management operations of Ohio, whereby information about rescue and lifesaving efforts is shared by all of the responding parties. So far Public Safety has developed the training program and identified instructors in a system aimed to prevent disastrous situations from becoming cataclysmic.

Another personnel initiative within Public Safety has made the uniformed force of the department more representative of Ohio's overall population. Governor Voinovich had said in his first Inaugural Address, "We must never forget that the infrastructure of good race relations and human understanding is more important than any roads or bridges we might build." Between the years 1991 and 1998, the numbers of minorities and women hired for the Highway Patrol rose from 16 percent to 24 percent (15 percent more minority and 9 percent more women). Of a total force by late 1998 of 1,376 in uniform, 207 are members of minority groups and 126 are women, according to department records.

PUBLIC UTILITIES COMMISSION (PUCO)

"We will put forth a comprehensive energy strategy to help keep the lid on energy and utility costs. I have taken a leadership role in trying to keep Southeast Ohio coal jobs and to keep down our utility rates," Governor Voinovich said in the 1991 State of the State Address. Before the Operations Improvement Task Force ever convened, much less drafted global recommendations, the governor was committed to investigating ways to reduce energy costs. By 1994 the Ohio Energy Strategy Task Force, chaired by PUCO, presented a report to the governor that detailed seven implementation strategies and fifty-three specific initiatives on energy use for citizens, private industry, and governments both state and local. Called the Ohio Energy Report, the document was compiled from more than 4,200 pages of comment recorded in public forums in twelve cities.

After the report was presented, another round of forums hosted by PUCO navigated the choppier waters of electric restructuring, which is jargon for the transformation of electric utility markets from monopolies into competitive situations. The specter of third-party suppliers selling power directly to end-use customers (called *wheeling*) motivated PUCO to devise an alternative that might balance the needs and interests of parties involved—meaning Ohio businesses as well as utility company shareholders and ratepayers. Conjunctive electric service (CES) is the term for aggregating different customer service locations for rates and billing. When PUCO assembled all the interested parties at quarterly Ohio Electric Roundtables, it recommended a CES pilot program to prevent any one party from gaining an unfair competitive advantage. Commercial customers with heavy electricity demands, such as grocery and restaurant chains, are especially interested in the CES approach to electric service. PUCO promoted another response to the possibilities raised by electric restructuring: the interruptible buy-through, which is an agreement between utility and customer to import power when the customer's service might be interrupted. Electric restructuring is far from resolved, despite PUCO's efforts at the Roundtables to head off litigation. Governor Voinovich's opinion was made clear in the 1997 State of the State Address: "But we must be aware of what the competition is doing. For example, surrounding states have taken steps toward 'retail wheeling' of electricity in order to lower energy costs for consumers—an action that could threaten Ohio's competitive position."

PUCO was also involved in developing customer choice programs in the natural gas industry. In addition to authorizing Ohio-based companies to provide alternative suppliers of gas to customers, the commission is implementing new legislation that permits gas companies to devise new rate methods for billing their customers. Guidelines for new telephone companies entering the marketplace were written by PUCO as well, in order to comply with the federal Telecommunications Act of 1996. In fact, Ohio was the first state to write a comprehensive guideline package for local telephone companies, which was cited by the Federal Communication Commission as a model to emulate. More than forty new telephone companies have been certified to compete in Ohio, according to PUCO documents.

DEPARTMENT OF TAXATION

Most of the changes in tax policy between 1991 and 1998 were focused on creating jobs for Ohioans and are appropriately discussed in the next chapter. But Taxation nevertheless played a role in the overall management of tax changes, beginning in 1993 with the Commission to Study the Ohio Economy and Tax Structure, or Tax Study Commission for short. Created by the General Assembly at Governor Voinovich's request, the group of fifteen citizens made recommendations after thorough study of data and history compiled by Taxation. It was the first such tax review since the 1970s, and was "long overdue," according to the governor. In addition to serving as a resource for the tax study, the department made its own changes for managing tax files. Affecting all tax operations was the Integrated Tax Administration System (ITAS), a computer titan that integrates all data, financial and nonfinancial, for a single taxpayer in one central account. For example, Business Owner Z can verify his or her tab in the areas of sales tax, corporate franchise tax, and withholding tax with one phone call. Taxation officials predict the ITAS will improve collections to the tune of $32 million.

The Department of Taxation initiated several improvements in the 1990s to make filing taxes faster and simpler not only for government but also for the taxpayer. The first of these was the 1040EZ form modeled after the federal version and introduced in 1993. Ohio's simplified form presents the taxpayer with four lines and one calculation. Fast Answers for State Taxes (FAST) allows taxpayers to get prerecorded answers (instead of a busy signal) to commonly asked tax questions. By 1998 the department fielded 970,792 calls compared to a pre-FAST total of about 200,000 per year. Two new filing methods dispense with traditional paper and pencil altogether. Telefile, begun in 1997, permits filing with a touch-tone telephone. In 1998

Ohio developed electronic filing via computer in conjunction with the Internal Revenue Service.

Another innovation by Taxation, one that won the department a national award in 1995, was the Managed Audit Program, which enables small and medium-sized businesses to conduct sales tax audits more simply. And for the larger businesses with headquarters outside Ohio, Taxation now has an office in New York to add to the Chicago and Los Angeles offices, which were expanded—all to reduce travel expenses by state employees paid for by taxpayers. It is safe to say that Taxation was motivated by the same OIT-inspired quest for quality that affected every state office in Columbus. But where taxes are concerned, surely words form the governor's 1991 State of the State Address hung in the air: "I see it as the governor's job to represent the taxpayers to government, not to represent government to taxpayers."

"I see it as the governor's job to represent the taxpayers to government, not to represent government to taxpayers."

DEPARTMENT OF TRANSPORTATION (ODOT)

While no person or activity in state government escaped the wide net of the OIT process during the Voinovich years, some units felt the reforms more than others did. The Department of Transportation (ODOT) is a prime example. Faced with a legislative mandate to reduce operating expenses by $108 million during 1996–97, coupled with OIT-instigated efficiency recommendations, ODOT's staff shrank from 7,800 to 6,500, a downsizing of 16.6 percent. Although it might seem to follow that motorists faced a mandate of downsized roads, according to department information, enough was saved from operating expenses in those two years to put major new construction projects in five counties on track. ODOT awarded $928 million in construction and maintenance contracts in 1997, which surpassed the average of $793 million produced between 1991 and 1996.

Part of the reason for the seeming anomaly of a decreased budget and increased construction is that Governor Voinovich put *federal* highway dollars to work harder. In his role as chairman of the National Governors' Association, Ohio's governor pushed for and got more highway dollars from Washington. Under the new Transportation Equity Act for the 21st Century, Ohio's share of federal money for highways is predicted to rise from $625 million to $896 million per year, according to data from the governor's Washington office. Though Ohio dollars sent to Washington don't return in high percentages on all fronts, the amount in highway dollars has improved measurably. In 1992, 79¢ of every federal highway dollar came back to Ohio. By 1998 the amount rose to 90.5¢. The 11.5¢ difference adds up to more millions of dollars over the years.

Just to get a feel for how those millions transform into asphalt and concrete, in 1997, 2,087 miles of Ohio roads were resurfaced at a cost of $264 million. That's enough to resurface the distance between Cleveland at one end of Ohio and Portsmouth on the other—nine times. New construction is another matter. It cost $207 million to build only 81.5 miles of new highway (the 1997 total), not even the distance between Columbus in mid-Ohio and Portsmouth one-way.

Decision making on ODOT projects was made more objective during the eight years of Governor Voinovich's tenure in a two-tiered management change. One tier was a four-year planning document called the Major New Construction Ranking Process, which incorporated traffic engineering data and economic development potential into decisions on which road would get built before another. In 1997 the decision making was further refined by legislative approval for the Transportation Review Advisory Council (TRAC), a seven-member body that adds public hearings to data in deciding which major projects will be funded. In addition to the ODOT director, who serves as chair, TRAC gets its members via appointment: four by the governor (with Senate approval), one by the House speaker, one by the Senate president. TRAC's procedures not only remove subjectivity from prioritizing road and bridge construction, but also add an oversight role to keep ODOT within budgets.

One other ODOT management tool added in 1996 by the General

Assembly was the Contract/Vendor Quality Bill, which lets the director exclude contractors and vendors, reject substandard products and services, and even demand warranties on material and work. Used extensively in Europe and tested by a few states in the USA, warranties give the ODOT director quality-control power to demand reimbursement of costs if ODOT has to perform maintenance work within five years of warranted construction.

Rather than rely solely on the customary increase in gasoline taxes, ODOT got a new revenue enhancement in 1997 in its cell tower agreement with the wireless communication industry. By charging a fee for use of the state-owned right-of-way on which relay towers stand, ODOT could add as much as $15 to $20 million to its coffers to fund construction projects.

Shades of OIT also color ODOT's merging of construction and maintenance functions at the county level. The position of county manager replaced that of county superintendent in a restructuring aimed to make the best use of 2,300 employees (one-third of ODOT's work force) who had previously worked under the dictates of the seasons—construction workers in summer and maintenance workers in winter, when snow and ice removal is job one. In order to expedite the integration of both construction and maintenance duties under a county manager, ODOT began cross-training workers in both tasks to improve year-round productivity. What's more, snow and ice removal may improve under a novel plan to designate six or seven snow and ice spotters (such as school superintendents and county sheriffs) in every county to evaluate the quality of ODOT's work, on a volunteer basis of course. In fact, Governor Voinovich's first Inaugural Address ended with a call for volunteerism: "Perhaps my greatest challenge as governor will be to convince every Ohioan that they are truly needed and that they can really make a difference. One organization, one group, one person can make a difference in someone's life."

"One organization, one group, one person can make a difference in someone's life."

CHAPTER 3

Jobs and Economic Development

"The people of Ohio understand that a good job is at the heart of the American dream."

WHEN GEORGE VOINOVICH took the oath of office as governor in 1991, Ohio was in the midst of a chain reaction of lost jobs, lost businesses, lost population, and lost Congressional seats. He said that day, "The people of Ohio understand that a good job is at the heart of the American dream." Then he spelled out the methods his administration would use to pursue jobs for Ohioans: "We must create a business environment that allows us to retain, expand, and attract more and better jobs. We must emphasize technology and the export of Ohio products into the global marketplace." Using those words from the 1991 Inaugural Address as a framework, this chapter takes a detailed look at actions that redeem the governor's pledge to make good jobs the heart of Ohio. He worked on all fronts—from workers' compensation that paid injured workers without injuring business profits, to welfare reform that edified jobs as the core goal for individuals, to tax incentives that coaxed new businesses to locate inside the state's borders, to itineraries abroad to court international trade, even to gladhanding travel writers who might speak well of his state. An agency-by-agency review of what was done on a smaller scale to get Ohioans into jobs, to get jobs into Ohio, and to get Ohio exports out follows the broader topics.

BUREAU OF WORKERS' COMPENSATION (BWC)

An unscientific survey of Ohioans is likely to name reform in workers' compensation as one of the top five of Governor Voinovich's major achievements in economic development during his eight-year gubernatorial tenure. The changes in Workers' Compensation could just as easily fit in the preceding chapter on Management, but given that Governor Voinovich himself called the workers' compensation system "a silent killer of jobs in Ohio," the topic segues logically into a discussion of Ohio's business climate. Since 1955 the bureau has existed as the financial arm of a safety net for workers injured on the job, whether temporarily or permanently. In addition to paying for workers' medical expenses, the state provides compensation to cover wages lost due to injuries. Before 1955, Ohio's Industrial Commission (IC) handled the entire compensation process. Created in 1913, the IC put the state squarely between workers and businesses as mediator, intending to circumvent the time and expense of potential litigation on every injury. But as industrialization burgeoned in Ohio and the caseload rose concomitantly, it became prudent to separate the functions of judgment and payment. In 1955 the BWC was anointed to handle the insurance, while the three-member IC retained its adjudication role of hearing claim disputes and ruling on safety violations. An independent BWC board was impaneled in 1989, ostensibly to depoliticize the workers' compensation apparatus. Size alone accounted for some of the urgency in reforming the BWC. Early in Governor Voinovich's first term, the BWC was collecting about $2 billion in premiums each year and investing reserves of more than $10 billion.

As Governor Voinovich said so bluntly in the 1992 State of the State Address, "The mess in Workers' Compensation has to be cleaned up. We can't ask Ohio employers to pay hundreds of dollars more [in premiums] than nearby competitors, or ask Ohio workers to go for months without money they are owed for injuries on the job. We now have a plan, the McKinsey Report, put together by this nation's premier management consultant, at no cost to the taxpayers. That report is now being converted into legislation." (Just to clarify the term, when the governor says *competitor*, he means the other forty-nine states in the USA.)

A report (actually McKinsey did two reports) by a respected company does not convert to law without some give and take. Nor do laws, once passed, convert to implementation overnight. Cleaning up the mess was messy. Rather than recite the developments as they unfolded chronologically, it might be helpful at the outset to distinguish among the beneficiaries as well as to categorize the changes in workers' compensation. First is the state itself as a management entity. Ohio benefited from (1) cost-cutting in medical and wage expenses and (2) changes in governance. Second is the employer group, whether public or private, which benefited from (3) decreased premium rates and increased credits and (4) incentives for safety. Third is the workforce, also referred to here as customers, who benefited from (5) improvements in customer service and (6) more rehabilitation and education, and of course the incentives for safety already mentioned. All three constituencies benefited from (7) aggressive efforts to stop fraud.

The legislature mandated managed care in the workers' compensation system in 1993, but it was not until 1997 that the Health Partnership Program (HPP) was fully implemented. Developed by the bureau, HPP is a private-sector managed-care system to provide health care to injured workers at an estimated 15 percent savings in medical and indemnity dollars over previous plans, according to BWC data. The 15 percent savings, when multiplied by the numbers of workers statewide covered by BWC, rapidly accrued zeros and commas in its total. The bureau also took a leadership role in the move toward a statewide Pharmacy Benefits Manager as a component of HPP. For the one-third of employees in Ohio not covered by BWC, a Quality Health Plan system was devised for self-insuring employers, those large and stable employers who meet BWC qualifications for the self-insurance designation.

In 1995 the responsibility for BWC administration passed from its independent board back to the governor. Shortly after Governor Voinovich named an administrator, he appointed members to the new nine-member Workers' Compensation Oversight Commission. One significant outcome of the administrative changes was a new investment policy. State insurance fund assets of $18 billion, invested in the bullish late 1990s under the more flexible policy, clearly contributed to premium credits for employers in 1997. Ohio also adopted national standards in its premium classifications. In 1996 the bureau began a four-year phase-in of the standards of the National Council on Compensation Insurance, whose models had been adopted by thirty-seven other states. One other administrative change was BWC's business consultant partnership with the Department of Development, whereby BWC experts in twelve regional economic development offices around the state deliver the message to new businesses about the overhauled workers' compensation bureau.

Changes in the premium rates can be conveyed meaningfully only by marshaling all the numbers that add up to savings for public and private employers, a total savings of more than $4 billion through a combination of premium rate reductions and annual credits between 1995 and 1998, according to numbers supplied by the Office of Budget and Management. The year-by-year changes followed this pattern: FY (fiscal year) 1996 rate reduction of 7.3 percent; FY 1997 rate reduction of 6 percent and premium credit of 20 percent; FY 1998 rate reduction of 15 percent and premium credit of 75 percent; FY 1999 rate reduction of 6 percent and a premium rebate package totaling $2 billion. Public employers (state and local governments and school districts) enjoyed similar rounds of rate reductions of 7.3

percent, 5 percent, and 10 percent. They, too, shared in the largess of the 1997 premium dividend credit of 75 percent. All those percentages of course represent millions, even billions, of dollars shifted from state accounts to the asset columns of employers. The fund surplus at the end of 1998 was $3.5 billion.

Safety is of course its own reward, but is now compensated as well with discounts and awards as incentives. The Premium Discount Program offers credits to employers with prior penalty ratings if they follow a ten-step plan to improve workplace safety. Multi-tiered premium discounts (ranging from 6 to 20 percent) are also available to employers who adopt a Drug-Free Workplace Program, a 1997 innovation partnered with the Department of Alcohol and Drug Addiction Services. In the first six months, 525 businesses had enrolled. In 1996 the first Governor's Excellence in Workers' Compensation Awards were presented to Ohio businesses and public employers in recognition of their safe but cost-effective workplaces.

September 1995 marked the debut of the BWC Office of Customer Service to serve as advocate for injured workers. A list of performance measures for the new office underscores its role to stay focused on providing injured workers with quality customer service. Next, town meetings began in November to gather information from employers and workers alike. To find out more about the needs and concerns of customers, several statewide surveys of injured workers and employers were conducted in early 1996. Several improvements in the process of filing claims followed the fact gathering. Eight claim applications were replaced with one. Ten toll-free telephone numbers were replaced with one number, conveniently accessed by dialing 1-800-OHIOBWC. A web site was added. Claim forms and the filing process were simplified. Brochures with clear explanations are now mailed to claimants in a matter of days, accompanied by two wallet-sized BWC identification cards, one to carry and one to file. Benefits can be transferred electronically to injured workers' accounts with a card that speeds up payment and bypasses the postal system. In his 1998 State of the State Address, Governor Voinovich summarized the effect of these improvements in the BWC filing process. "We have cut delays in the reporting of workers' injuries by 48 percent."

The Bureau of Workers' Compensation has always been in the business of promoting rehabilitation and safety education in the form of seminars and workshops. BWC has added a national conference on workers' compensation and safety, held in Columbus in mid-September 1998.

An intensified crackdown on fraud is another arena in which BWC saves money. Bear in mind that perpetrators of claim fraud lurk among medical providers, workers, and employers alike. As of 1997, the state may prosecute those charged with fraud. One innovation created by a QStP team let BWC's Special Investigations Department implement an automated fraud referral process from claims representatives. A more dramatic technique, reminiscent of movieland stings, was Operation Longarm, which identified $2.9 million in fraud after locating cheats in Florida, Georgia, and Tennessee via information shared with counterpart agencies in those states. The total saved by fending off fraud in 1997 was $52 million, an increase of almost 50 percent over the prior year, according to BWC figures. Because fighting fraud costs money, BWC tracks that cost, too. In fiscal 1997 the Special Investigations Department saved $5.74 for every dollar spent. As for medical providers who attempted to defraud the state in 1997, BWC got $19 million of the state's money back after verifying that certain medical services were never actually performed.

"Our administration decided that helping to empower families and eliminating the barriers that impede self-sufficiency are our greatest obligations. We understand that when families succeed, Ohio succeeds."

FROM WELFARE REFORM TO "OHIO WORKS FIRST"

In the 1996 State of the State Address Governor Voinovich expressed his philosophy on the relationship between government and families: "Our administration decided that helping to empower families and eliminating the barriers that impede self-sufficiency are our greatest obligations. We understand that when families succeed, Ohio succeeds. We also understand that, while many families do not need or want anything from government, a great many others are struggling. We have tried to avoid the mistakes of the federal government, which for the last thirty years has tried unsuccessfully to substitute itself for the family. We look to personal responsibility and to our extended family of communities, churches, schools, and other organizations that support families, which I think do a lot better job than we do."

Little wonder that Governor Voinovich did not wait for the federal government to clear the way for welfare reform. As early as 1992 he embarked on the elimination of General Assistance, Ohio's public assistance program for able-bodied adults. The underlying principle was simple—self-sufficiency, to put people into jobs. Taking the place of GA was the Disability Assistance (DA) program for individuals whose disabling conditions prevented their working. In 1995 alone, 94,000 adults stopped receiving GA cash benefits, saving the state $275 million by the administration's calculations in December of that year.

Self-sufficiency was only one plank of the governor's welfare reform platform. A pro-family philosophy was another. As the governor said in January 1995, "We must also restructure those aspects of our current welfare system that are anti-family. Toward that end, we will do away with the financial disincentive for ADC mothers who marry, and the 100-hour work rule, which also discourages work for two-parent families." In later speeches the governor praised the bipartisan effort that culminated in the August passage of the 1995 welfare reform law in Ohio (House Bill 167). Key features of the bill were time limits on receiving assistance, incentives and help to encourage the transition to self-sufficiency, and restoration of the sanctity of the family—all of which would reappear more firmly codified in the 1997 welfare reform bill called "Ohio Works First."

Time magazine called the governor's plan "one of the most intelligent in the nation." Governor Voinovich called it a new system that "treats people, not like statistics, but as God's children—most of whom desperately want a fighting chance to raise their families, become successful, and make a contribution to society. It is our responsibility to give them that chance."

Perhaps because Governor Voinovich had pioneered reform, he had the ear of House and Senate leaders who were writing the federal reform package. The governor wanted to increase Ohio's funding level, to guard against mandates, and to instate a rainy day fund for human services to protect states from the vicissitudes of economic recessions. He got all three.

Between the Ohio welfare reform laws of 1995 and 1997 were federal changes universally assumed to be a foregone conclusion, until President Bill Clinton vetoed Congress's legislation in January 1996. Hanging in the balance were waivers (federal permission slips) Ohio needed to proceed with many of its reforms. It took seven months to get waivers that had been promised within thirty days, and approval was withheld for some aspects of Ohio's welfare reform. After federal legislation did pass in the summer of 1996 (the Personal Responsibility and Work Opportunity Reconciliation Act), Ohio lawmakers got busy redesigning welfare according to the new stipulations, which positioned Ohio to get a $728 million-per-year block grant from Washington titled Temporary Assistance for Needy Families (TANF), which replaced ADC. Important to the welfare reform story is that TANF amounts to the states were tied to the early 1990s, when Ohio had its largest number of welfare recipients. Lawmakers also incorporated information gleaned from a series of public meetings in Ohio counties and from focus group sessions with welfare recipients before finalizing details of reform.

The refurbished welfare law, christened Ohio Works First (OWF), was signed by Governor Voinovich on July 2, 1997. It incorporated six principles that have guided the reform effort from the beginning:

1. Help people achieve and maintain employment.

2. Maximize the self-sufficiency of the economically vulnerable.

3. Support the needs of the families of children and promote family stability.

4. Focus on the prevention of long-term dependence.

5. Emphasize personal responsibility.

6. Include a statewide minimum core set of services.

What the principles don't communicate is that Ohio Works First also broke with tradition in the realm of administration. County commissioners and their county departments of human services would take primary responsibility for developing and implementing assistance programs. That is, the state handed over to counties not only the wherewithal to run with the program, but the autonomy to run their own pattern, too.

Here's how Ohio Works First works. The state Department of Human Services and each county Board of Commissioners sign a partnership agreement in which the former specifies its level of commitment (i.e., how much money to give) and the latter specifies performance expectations, or outcomes. Counties can earn more money by meeting performance goals, such as a certain level of work participation by welfare recipients. Counties are also expected to design programs that prevent families from needing the TANF cash. Called prevention/retention contingency services, examples may be something as obvious as car repair in order for a client to get to work. Twenty-two counties got under way with their partnership agreements in 1998. All eighty-eight counties will be phased in by January 2000. In the meantime, the federal block grants known as TANF provide a pool of cash for those who need it while everyone is adjusting to the new procedures. It should be noted, too, that counties that reduce the amount spent on TANF can retain a portion of those savings, just one of the incentive features that are a hallmark of Ohio

Works First. The state, meanwhile, had planned its own reserve fund for unspent TANF dollars, a fund that held $158 million by the end of FY 1998, according to OBM data, with FY 1999 projections of $330 million in reserve.

On to recipients. All OWF adults are required to work at least 30 hours per week. Adults in a two-parent household must work at least 35 hours per week, 55 hours if child care is provided. If an adult does not actually draw a paycheck, that person must participate in an approved "work activity." Up to 10 hours of the 30 may be devoted to educational or developmental needs. One example is the Local Linkages project partnered by the departments of Alcohol and Drug Addiction Services and Human Services, providing education and treatment for those with addictions. Alternatives are assigned to those adults who cannot participate in traditional work or related activities. Some examples of alternatives are parenting classes, life skills training, and participation in alcohol or drug addiction prevention programs. The number of work hours increases over the next five years. At the outset, every recipient must sign a Self-Sufficiency Contract, which is a plan to achieve long-term self-sufficiency without subsidies. The contract lists all the obligations the recipient must fulfill and all the support services he or she will receive. Assisting recipients at this point are various job-seeking and job-training programs. Failure to fulfill contract terms will result in loss of benefits.

One of the more radical departures of OWF from traditional welfare is the time limit. Recipients may receive cash benefits for three years maximum. After that, they must sit out for two years and receive no cash, after which they may apply for an additional two years of assistance if they can show good cause. The clock started ticking on these time limits October 1, 1997. One major benefit other than cash is the Medicaid eligibility available to all TANF cash recipients.

A pro-family set of regulations is another innovation. Most significant is the expansion of Medicaid eligibility to include children through age eighteen for those families under 150 percent of the federal poverty level. Furthermore, child care is available for most OWF families who are participating in work activities. OWF participants under order to pay child support must pay it—period. OWF families who abuse or neglect a child who is subsequently removed from the home must enter into a plan for reunification in order to receive TANF benefits for up to ninety days. Last, teenage parents must live at home or in an adult-supervised setting in order to receive OWF benefits. Funding for such support services does cost money. For example, the child care budget has grown from $37 million in 1991 to more than $250 million in the 1999 budget. However, as people leave the welfare rolls and unspent TANF accumulates, states may use it to cover any and all costs associated with moving people into jobs. In return for those dollars spent, 80,000 Ohio children are cared for while their parents work or train for work. In addition, recipients are still entitled to federal food stamps, for which the rules have been simplified to be consistent with OWF eligibility.

One last change pertains to immigrants who arrived in the United States after August 22, 1996. They must live in the U.S. for five years before they become eligible for benefits. Illegal immigrants are not eligible at any time.

Ohio Works First is too new for many conclusions to be drawn. However, a few figures do illustrate the outcomes of welfare changes since Governor Voinovich took office. From March 1992 when caseloads peaked at 750,000 recipients (including ADC, GA, and DA), the state's caseload has dropped to about 249,000 at the end of 1998. According to OBM figures, the caseload reductions have saved the state $1.268 billion.

One conclusion can be drawn without benefit of numbers. Implementing OWF requires all county agencies to work closely together to aid individuals whom several social service agencies may be serving simultaneously as clients. Even nongovernmental agencies are brought into the collaboration to become part of the "extended family" the governor envisioned as a better support system for families than a faraway central government. In Southeastern Ohio, for example, several different organizations that aid the transition from welfare to work cooperate with the county departments of human services. To name one, Community Foods Initiatives (CFI) is a grass-roots organization of people interested in food production and processing as a means to self-sufficiency. Volunteers from a host of sources staffed these social service organizations before Ohio Works First was ever drafted. Yet the passage of OWF in 1997 made state agencies look at the grassroots organizations in a new light—as partners working together.

ECONOMIC DEVELOPMENT FOR INDIVIDUAL TAXPAYERS

Much of the ensuing discussion will pivot on tax policy, introduced as a management topic in the Department of Taxation section on the Tax Study Commission in Chapter 2. While the tax study was a management concern, its outcomes materialized as economic development for individuals as well as businesses, given that individual taxpayers view tax cuts as an improvement in their personal finances. Tax cuts were made possible by surplus year-end balances in the General Revenue Fund, some of which went into the Rainy Day Fund, while some enabled tax relief in two forms: personal exemption increases and rate cuts. Summary data from the Office of Budget and Management set the total savings to state income taxpayers between 1994 and 1999 at $1.8 billion.

The personal exemption represents real money to taxpayers, as that amount is removed from taxable income and thereby lowers the tax owed to the government. Reasoning that years of inflation had eroded the impact of the static personal exemption, the governor and legislature approved stepped increases beginning in 1996. The precise personal exemption for a taxpayer and spouse in tax year 1999 will be $1050, compared to $650 in tax year 1995. The exemption for dependents reached $1,050 in tax year 1997.

A rate cut of 6.61 percent took effect for 1996 and a 3.99 percent rate reduction applied in 1997, both in order to return accumulated

GRF surpluses totaling $660 million in the Income Tax Reduction Fund. The 1996 rate cut converted to $400.8 million returned to taxpayers, while the 1997 dollar return total was $262.9 million. When taxpayers file their 1998 taxes, the dollar total returned to them will be $701.4 million, thanks to the budget surplus on June 30, 1997. That represents a 9.3 percent tax cut for Ohioans.

Four other tax reductions helped some state taxpayers. Two are deductions and two are credits. The Homestead Exemption income cap was raised in 1995, which increased the number of people 65 or older eligible for a property tax reduction of $300. An additional 9,000 older Ohioans took the exemption in 1995. The income eligibility cap was increased from $16,500 to $20,800, which means that individuals whose income is below the latter figure are now eligible for the exemption. (The act establishing the Homestead Exemption for senior citizens had been introduced in the late 1960s by Rep. George Voinovich.) Self-employed individuals who buy their own health insurance can deduct the amount paid for health care premiums from their income, starting in 1993. Tax credits, those boons subtracted from the "tax due" amount, can be taken by individuals who lose their jobs due to plant closings; half of the amount spent on job training within twelve months of losing their jobs may be taken as a credit, up to $500. The state tax rules for child care also lightened the tax burden for some. Before 1997 eligible Ohioans could take only 35 percent of the federal tax credit as a state tax credit for dependent care. Now those taxpayers can take 100 percent of the federal credit, if their adjusted gross income is less than $20,000. For individuals whose AGI is between $20,000 and $40,000, the state income tax credit for child care is 25 percent of the federal credit.

ECONOMIC DEVELOPMENT FOR BUSINESS TAXPAYERS

The Office of Budget and Management compiled a list of business tax incentives that are the epicenter of the Voinovich administration's efforts to maintain and expand jobs in Ohio. Though the incentives were phased in under separate pieces of legislation called Jobs Bills I, II, and III, the centerpiece of all three bills is the list of tax deductions and tax credits that make Ohio attractive to businesses. Solid data justify use of the word *attractive*. For three of the four years up to 1997, Ohio was ranked number one in the nation by *Site Selection and Industrial Development* magazine for highest number of new facilities, expanded facilities, and new manufacturing plants. The total number of jobs generated by new or expanded operations for 1996, for example, is 27,000, or roughly the population of Zanesville. It's also instructive to back away from the one-year frame to the larger picture. The total number of jobs created between January 1, 1991, and July 1998 is 541,000, or about the population of Cleveland. In fact, Governor Voinovich was so encouraged by results only two years after the passage of Jobs Bill I that he declared in the 1994 State of the State Address, "Ladies and gentlemen, the rust is off the belt!"

> *"Ladies and gentlemen, the rust is off the belt!"*

One of the incentives that drew businesses to Ohio was the Job Creation Tax Credit. By this process, a corporation enters into an agreement with the Tax Credit Authority. A contract specifies a percentage of Ohio income tax withheld on new employees to be designated as the credit, usually 50 to 75 percent. That is, if the total of Ohio income tax withheld on the new employees in a given year is $100,000, the credit can be anywhere from $50,000 to $75,000. The credit for the year is then applied to the business's corporate franchise tax for the year. Whatever percentage the business agrees to in the initial contract with the Tax Credit Authority is permitted for a period up to ten years. According to OBM data, 613 companies were approved to receive this tax credit between 1993 and October 1998. The combined investment total of the 613 companies was $7.6 billion, which created 67,640 jobs and retained 100,000 jobs. The tax credit total awarded by the state was $220 million.

The Job Creation Tax Credit was not the only thing good to happen to the corporate franchise tax in Ohio during the Voinovich years. In 1997 an overhaul to the franchise tax *per se* implemented the findings of the Tax Study Commission. In essence, the tax was dysfunctionally complex and required too much record keeping. The corporate franchise tax revision simplified the net worth component, lowered the tax rate, and capped liability, among other changes. Another opportunity to lower corporate franchise tax liability was the Export Tax Credit, which is applicable to tax years 1993 through 2005. To gain this tax advantage, a business must show that its export sales increased (along with a simultaneous increase in Ohio payroll taxes or capital expenditures). Though the calculation is complex, the credit is roughly 10 percent of the increased profits derived from increased exports. The credit maximum is $250,000 per year, which can be carried forward to future years.

Some of the new tax incentives dealt with installing or retooling machinery and equipment, including technology. Investment tax credits on new manufacturing machinery and equipment were enacted in 1994, 1995, and 1996. The 1994 rule set a credit equal to 20 percent of the cost of the new machinery and equipment so long as three conditions were met: (1) the new equipment was located in Ohio; (2) the cost of the new purchases equaled or exceeded 20 percent of the cost of the taxpayer's total tangible property in the U.S. at the end of the preceding tax year; and (3) the purchases were made between January 1, 1995, and June 30, 1996. That is, if a businessperson owned $5 million in property anywhere in the nation, that person had to spend at least $1 million on new machinery and equipment within the specified eighteen months and locate it in Ohio before becoming eligible for a 20 percent credit of $200,000. The maximum credit of $500,000 may be carried forward for up to three years. A similar credit was enacted in 1996 but with a shorter period for making purchases and lower investment threshold. The 1995 law on investment credit for machinery and equipment added two new variables to eligibility—reinvestment within the same county and location in economically depressed areas. If purchases of manufacturing machinery and equipment represented an increase in investment within the same county, the taxpayer was eligible for a tax credit of 7.5 percent of the cost of the new purchases. The new purchases must fall between July 1, 1995, and December 31, 2000, and the prior investments are computed on an average invested between 1992 through 1994. A higher percentage, 13.5 percent, applies if the investment is made in an area characterized as distressed or with a labor surplus.

In order to encourage the start-up of businesses engaged in research and development or technology transfer, a Technology Investment Credit was passed in 1996 that is equal to 25 percent of the investment, so long as it is approved by the state Industrial Technology and Enterprise Board. The higher maximum on this particular credit—$10 million—reflects the costs of such investment.

Removing potential environmental hazards from abandoned manufacturing sites was the impetus for the Brownfields Cleanup Credits. Passed in 1996, the corporate franchise tax credit for costs incurred in voluntary cleanup of contaminated sites may be taken by those corporations who enter an agreement with the director of the Department of Development. The value of the credit is the lesser amount of $500,000 or 10 percent of cleanup costs or the lesser amount of $750,000 or 15 percent if the site location is in a priority investment area. Other incentives for Brownfields Cleanup include real and personal property tax abatements (passed in 1994) and low-interest loans as well as grants.

Some of the changes in tax reform to stimulate economic development were focused on particular types of business—insurance, financial institutions, and telecommunications. A potentially unconstitutional preference for domestic insurance companies was noted in the Tax Study Commission's report. In short, Ohio-based companies paid less than those headquartered outside the state. In addition, certain health maintenance organizations had been exempt from paying insurance taxes. Both these inequities will be corrected with a new rate structure that phases in over five years beginning in FY 1999. Under the new rates, non-health insurance premiums are taxed at 1.4 percent and health insurance premiums are taxed at 1 percent. The very definition of a financial institution had to change in Ohio in order to synchronize with a 1997 federal law that eased movement across state lines for these companies. Like the rules in insurance, Ohio's tax structure for financial institutions had favored in-state companies. Also, the tax rates for financial institutions will be lowered beginning in 1999 in order to bolster Ohio's position as a business center. Fairness and a court ruling motivated the governor and General Assembly to square property taxes for telecommunications companies with the rates for general business operations. The assessed value of property used by long-distance telephone companies was therefore reduced from 88 percent to 25 percent, with a battery of stipulations to cover variations in year of establishment within Ohio.

One particular tax incentive for business worked in concert with the governor's efforts to move welfare recipients into jobs. The Enterprise Zone Subsidized Employment Credit, passed in 1994, gives a tax break to qualified corporations that locate in enterprise zones, which is a term for disadvantaged areas. Ohio has about three hundred enterprise zones. For each new employee who is also receiving benefits under TANF (formerly known as Aid to Families with Dependent Children), enterprise zone corporations may take a maximum credit of $1,000. Credit in excess of tax due may be carried forward for three years.

The governor was pleased enough with the tax incentives to cite them in the 1998 State of the State Address. "Through our landmark series of jobs bills, we've transformed Ohio's incentive package into one that states across the country are still scrambling to copy. Today, all of these efforts are paying major dividends for the people of Ohio."

SELLING OHIO—PUBLIC APPEARANCES BOTH FOREIGN AND DOMESTIC

The governor himself made sales calls abroad to promote the purchase of Ohio products by foreign nations. He also crisscrossed the state to familiarize travel writers with Ohio's stellar tourist attractions. In the foreign and domestic travel, the governor pursued not only good will, but also measurable sales and column inches for Ohio.

In his 1992 State of the State Address, Governor Voinovich issued a call to arms on exports. He went on to explain that increased exports of Ohio goods and services create new jobs for Ohioans. "But we also need to help educate Ohio businesses on how to build their export trade, and we need a vehicle to showcase the quality of Ohio products to potential customers worldwide." The headmaster in this school to teach exporting was George Voinovich, who had long advocated learning about international competition, and that those businesspeople who didn't would "wake up and find their market share gone."

"We need a vehicle to showcase the quality of Ohio products to potential customers worldwide."

In 1992 Governor and Mrs. Voinovich led the first of nine Ohio Business, Trade, and Investment Missions accompanied by business leaders and state officials, all with the common goal of opening new markets for Ohio products. Summary data compiled by the Ohio Department of Development show that a total of 175 Ohio companies participated in the nine trips, which generated nearly half a billion dollars in new business, with another three-quarters of a billion dollars under negotiation as quotations or bids-in-process as of June 1998. For specific nations, exports of Ohio products have increased between 1991 and 1996 from as little as 12.7 percent in Israel to as much as 275 percent in Argentina. Trade with perennial customer Canada, top buyer of Ohio products, increased 88.9 percent from 1991 to 1996. The overall figure was the governor's to announce in the 1998 State of the State Address: "Between 1991 and 1996, Ohio's export of manufactured goods increased an unprecedented 48 percent."

The following sample illustrates only a portion of what Ohio has to sell to the world. Among the participants in the 1994 trip to Mexico were a manufacturer of metal stampings, gaskets, and wire forms; a manufacturer of sewer cleaning equipment; an organization with services for developing, managing, and commercializing technology; international legal services; a host of manufacturers in the automotive industry; a manufacturer of hoists, cranes, and winches; and eight agribusinesses producing goods from Christmas trees to corn chips.

A review of the itineraries illustrates that Ohio's sales region covers the globe. The first mission in 1992 was to Southeast Asia and included the nations of Thailand, Singapore, Malaysia, Indonesia, Hong Kong, and Japan. In 1993 the Ohioans went to Central and Eastern Europe in April with meetings in Austria, Slovenia, Slovak Republic, Hungary, Czech Republic, and Germany and to Israel in November, followed by a trip to Mexico in April 1994. Two trips were made in 1995, to the People's Republic of China and Hong Kong in April and back to Germany, Austria, and Slovenia in October. The sales target in 1996 was India. For 1997 the objective was the Pacific Rim nations of South Korea, Taiwan, and Australia. The last mission was to South America in 1998 and took in Argentina, Brazil, and Chile. Governor and Mrs. Voinovich were at the forefront of every mission to establish contacts and explore business linkages in leading markets. In fact, the governor tallied 275 meetings with business and government officials.

The travels, though, were intended only as opening gambits to sustained efforts to increase business abroad. Other teachers in the exporting school were experts in Ohio's international trade offices. Four new offices—Johannesburg, Mexico City, Tel Aviv, and Sao Paulo—were added to the four operating before 1991—Tokyo, Hong Kong, Toronto, and Brussels. The trade offices provide Ohio companies with local market research and contacts with agents, distributors, and end-users in those markets. Information to help the potential exporter from Ohio is also available at trade shows, trade missions, and the worldwide web. Ohio's online International Trade Directory puts businesspeople in touch with state officials, who in turn provide leads on establishing trade and expertise about issues in other nations such as distribution practices, political and economic stability, and language and cultural differences, to name a few. Another form of state assistance to businesses wishing to try their hand at exporting is the Ohio Export Finance Initiative (OEFI), which assists in arranging financing through a partnership between Ohio and the Export/Import Bank of the United States. Between 1993 and 1997, the ExImBank assisted 286 Ohio companies that aimed for global markets, according to figures from the Department of Development.

In addition to the nine trips abroad in eight years, Governor and Mrs. Voinovich participated in all or part of nineteen separate tours at home, trips to Ohio attractions called Familiarization Tours, or Fam Tours for short. Designed to attract top travel writers to Ohio, who might have been less inclined to visit the state if the host were a person of lesser rank than governor, the Fam Tours drew more than 150 writers and editors from the United States, Canada, and other nations. According to estimates by the Division of Travel and Tourism within the Department of Development, the tours generated media coverage worth $3 million had the space been paid for with advertising dollars. The publicity in the editorial columns is of course free. More importantly, content in the editorial sections of media carries a credibility that overt persuasion attempts often lack, especially in their paid forms. Though national and international travel guides list Ohio's widely known sites, such as the Rock 'n Roll Hall of Fame in Cleveland or the Statehouse in Columbus, not as many travel books include the less familiar places worth visiting in Ohio. A sampling from the Fam Tours includes the caves and waterfalls of the Hocking Hills, villages like Granville and Lebanon, and the City of Marietta, which holds singular status in both Ohio and American history.

Governor Voinovich's ideas were manifested in other initiatives to create new jobs and to boost economic development in various agency-specific ways. Descriptions follow, in alphabetical order of the agency of origination.

DEPARTMENT OF AGRICULTURE

Loss of farmland isn't unique to Ohio, but the numbers are stark. Between 1954 and 1992 more than 25 percent of Ohio's farmland, or 5.7

million acres, was converted to non-farm use, according to data from the Department of Agriculture. In 1996 Governor Voinovich appointed the Ohio Farmland Preservation Task Force to study the situation and devise incentives to stop the loss of productive acreage. The group issued its report in June 1997. One recommendation of the task force that was implemented right away was creation of the Office of Farmland Preservation within the Department of Agriculture to coordinate statewide efforts to retain farms. Many of the task force recommendations require legislation to implement, and work is underway to draft and sponsor appropriate bills. One bill has already emerged as law—the Family Farmer Loan Guarantee Program, which took effect in August 1998. As its name implies, the law helps family farmers get low-interest loans from private banks to purchase land, buildings, and stationary equipment to start or improve a farm.

Governor Voinovich used his authority to move one recommendation to action in January 1998 when he signed the Farmland Protection Executive Order, which directed state agencies to take into account farmland preservation goals in making land-use decisions. Another recommendation already actualized is the Agri-Industry Development Council, which is a consortium of agribusiness leaders and experts in both public and private domains. A partnership between the state departments of Agriculture and Development linked government officials with agri-industry leaders. The Council advocates for the interest of farmers beyond the issue of acreage by advising the administration on agricultural economic development.

Promoting the sale of Ohio agricultural products abroad was the job of the Department of Development until 1991, when the Department of Agriculture got its own International Trade Division. In the effort to open new markets for Ohio's agricultural products around the world, Governor Voinovich included agribusiness leaders in his overseas trade missions. From 1991 to 1997 sales of agricultural exports from Ohio increased from $1 billion to $1.6 billion. On the home front, the department initiated the OHIO PROUD program in 1993 to provide marketing support for products grown or processed in Ohio. As of September 1998, the program had grown to 184 business partners from 59 Ohio counties who work with the department in planning promotions. One specific tool used to spotlight Ohio products is the use of banners and shelf tags in major supermarkets. More than 25,000 tags appear statewide. A survey measuring the impact of the promotions showed an increase in awareness of the OHIO PROUD program. Twenty-six percent of those polled said they were aware of the program in 1997, up from 19 percent in 1996. Of those who were aware of the program, 38 percent reported that they look for the OHIO PROUD logo when they shop.

Ohio's livestock industry gained from three actions during the Voinovich administration. In order to attract national livestock shows, the state approved an $8.5 million facility named the Voinovich Livestock and Trade Center at the Ohio Expositions Center. The Agriculture Department also provides a livestock show incentive in the form of cost-sharing funds for national shows. One of these is the Ohio Beef Expo, which is the fifth largest convention in Columbus, according to department information. In another move to revitalize Ohio's livestock industry, the Governor's Packing Plant Task Force, formed in 1992, developed an eleven-point action plan to encourage the retention and expansion of Ohio packing plants.

Meat inspection was also the ground for a skirmish between the state of Ohio and the United States. With the aid of Ohio State Attorney General Betty D. Montgomery and the meat packing industry, the Ohio Department of Agriculture filed suit against the United States Department of Agriculture (USDA) in early 1997 to overturn the federal ban on the interstate sale of meat from state-inspected plants. The federal posture effectively declares the meat inspection procedures of the states inferior to its own. In the words of Ohio Department of Agriculture documents, the issue "has nothing to do with food safety and everything to do with federal interference in Ohio commerce." The state then commissioned a study by Ohio State University. Among the findings, "If the federal government would drop its restriction on interstate sales of state-inspected meat, 588 new jobs and $56.5 million would be added to Ohio's economy." Bolstered with these data, officials from the department testified at two hearings of the USDA. Other states' departments of agriculture concurred with Ohio in the argument against the federal ban. The lawsuit, economic data, and reinforcements from fellow states may have worked. In September 1997 and again in January 1998, the USDA issued position papers stating an interest in dropping the federal ban by the year 2000.

Combat was also waged in the courts on behalf of Ohio grain farmers. This time the contest ended in the U.S. Supreme Court in 1997. At stake were $3.2 million of the farmers' money and $2.8 million of the state's money in its Grain Indemnity Fund. The State of Ohio defended 172 farmers and other depositors against a bankrupt grain elevator in three different courts before Ohio won six years later. As a result, the Grain Warehouse Law was amended in 1998 to strengthen the financial requirements of licensed agricultural commodity handlers. To be brief, the Ohio Department of Agriculture, by state law, ensures that grain elevators have enough cash or grain reserves to cover the value of grain deposited by farmers. In the event of a facility's insolvency, producers are reimbursed by the state via the Grain Indemnity Fund.

DEPARTMENT OF COMMERCE

Ohio law caught up with federal law in a bill that aided economic development for banks in 1997. Called the Interstate Branching Bill, the law permits state chartered financial institutions to cross state lines to establish branches, as of June 1, 1997. Ohio banks may also merge with and acquire branches of banks headquartered in other states. Passage of the law was essential to keep Ohio banks competitive. Federal legislation passed in 1994 enabled national banks to expand across state lines whether or not the banks were part of a bank holding company. The effective date for the national law is also June 1, 1997.

DEPARTMENT OF DEVELOPMENT

It's a given that the department devoted to development was one of the workhorses in economic development, and many of its accomplishments have already been covered as major initiatives directed or monitored by the governor. But there is more to Development's efforts than the myriad tax incentives it promotes. Chief among these is the follow-through on the governor's promise to regionalize the department into twelve separate offices, each with a regional development representative and an administrative assistant who assist communities with local priorities. Locations of the twelve offices are Columbus, Toledo, Lima, Dayton, Cincinnati, Mansfield, Chillicothe, Cleveland, Akron, Cambridge, Marietta, and Youngstown. Accomplishment of this feat by 1993 allowed the governor to cite statistics of praise in his State of the State Address. "We're also very proud of the hard work being done in our twelve regional development offices around the state. Collectively, these offices worked on 212 major economic development projects in 1992, assisting in such victories as the new truck line at Toledo's Chrysler/Jeep plant that helped retain 5,500 jobs; the new Meijer's project in Tipp City near Dayton, with its 1,500 new jobs; and the huge Procter and Gamble research facility in Warren County, with its 1,800 jobs."

New enterprises in the Travel and Tourism Division, beyond the Fam Tours led by Governor and Mrs. Voinovich, brought tourist dollars into Ohio. Most notable is the partnership forged with advertisers in the private sector who now underwrite millions of dollars of the division's advertising. Comparative numbers tell the story. In 1991 the tourism advertising budget, funded by the division using taxpayer dollars from the General Revenue Fund, was $900,000. In 1998 the amount of advertising placed by Travel and Tourism was $7.1 million, $6 million of that from advertising partners in the private sector, according to division documents.

What may be a measure of the effectiveness of the messages created by those advertisers is the number of phone calls to 1-800-

BUCKEYE, the state's information line on tourist attractions. From 1991 to 1997 the volume of calls doubled, from 600,000 to 1.2 million. According to Travel and Tourism records, 1-800-BUCKEYE has the nation's highest call volume, even though Ohio ranks twenty-eighth in the nation in dollars allocated for its tourism budget. Seeking information is only one step in the travel process, though. The division has also compiled records showing that 70 percent of the people who call 1-800-BUCKEYE and order tourism information eventually do travel to Ohio. When that "action" figure is paired with call volume, it becomes clear that call volume is indeed one way to predict how many people might spend their money in Ohio. The state also saves money in its pursuit of tourists' dollars by contracting with prison labor to ship the tourism packets to people who have requested information via the toll-free information line. As the section on the Department of Rehabilitation and Correction explains later in this chapter, penal industry not only provides work and job training for those incarcerated, but also saves the state money. In the case of the tourism information packets, the amount saved annually since the partnership with the Chillicothe Correctional Institute began in 1994 has been $280,000.

Partnerships are also the vehicle for a new venture in Travel and Tourism to promote Ohio abroad. Two campaign consortia have been developed, one among states that share Great Lakes shorelines, the other with Ohio's Appalachian neighbors. The Great Lakes of North America (GLNA) group promotes tours of the region in English- and German-speaking parts of Europe. By 1998 the group had placed more than six million brochures in travel agencies in the United Kingdom and German-speaking nations. GLNA is funded and operated by state tourism offices in Ohio, Indiana, Michigan, Illinois, Minnesota, Wisconsin, and the Canadian province of Ontario and posts representatives in London and Dusseldorf. The marketing effort to the south uses federal dollars from the Appalachian Regional Commission to promote tours of the Appalachian Mountain and River Region of America. Begun in 1996 by counties in Ohio,

West Virginia, and Kentucky, the package is being featured by tour operators in Germany, Switzerland, and Austria.

Other achievements of the Travel and Tourism Division during the Voinovich years deserve mention. One is economizing in the publication of *OhioPass*, the primary travel magazine of the division. In 1991, 500,000 copies of the booklet were paid for with $300,000 from the division's budget. Seven years later, 800,000 copies were printed at no cost to the division because it had shifted to selling advertising, which now funds *OhioPass* entirely. Another is the money-making opportunity the division tapped by permitting buy-ins to its market research. A third new activity with potential to attract tourist money to Ohio is the division's chairing of the Heritage of Ohio Tourism Task Force, which is developing "heritage corridors" (e.g., canal corridors, Underground Railroad corridors) that may eventually draw federal dollars to promote trips with historical themes.

Elsewhere in the Department of Development, other efforts were undertaken on behalf of businesses wishing to locate in Ohio. In order to assist the newcomers in handling physical details of moving to Ohio, the Office of Business Development (OBD) linked certain services for clients with the clients' creation of new jobs. The Roadwork Development Account pays for certain road projects necessary for business start-up or expansion. Roadwork awards during the Voinovich years were made for 315 projects that the department projected would create or retain a total of more than 78,000 jobs. A similar OBD award program pays for such infrastructure improvements as water, sewer, and storm sewer systems. Called the Business Development Account, the fund in eight years subsidized 330 projects that were connected to the creation or retention of more than 98,000 jobs. The state also helps businesses locate their physical plants via a computer database compiled in 1997 called the Site Selection System, which can answer questions about available sites and buildings instantaneously. One method of assistance initiated during the Voinovich administration was to provide a helping hand through the bureaucratic maze. The Office of Business Development now has staff liaisons who work directly with new businesses in the regulatory areas of environment, agri-industry, workers' compensation, and transportation.

The Thomas Alva Edison Program, under the aegis of the Technology Division of the Department of Development, was designed to boost economic development by bringing together experts in technology from state, industry, and academia. Seven centers around the state act as clearinghouses for the latest research and methods in such fields as biotechnology, fiber optical communication systems, polymer applications, and metallurgical innovations, to name some of the better known.

Praising the Edison Program in his first State of the State Address, Governor Voinovich said, "We are going to build on this program and make Ohio a gigantic research park by tying together our universities, our research centers, and our businesses. Ohio was the touchstone of the Industrial Revolution in America at the turn of the 20th Century. I see no reason why we cannot be the touchstone of the technological revolution that will surely usher in the 21st Century." To that end, he sent his tech revolutionaries after non-state funds, mostly from industrial and federal sources, to expand the capabilities of the seven Edison Technology Centers.

Narrower in scope than the centers are the nine Edison Incubators, which function to nurture smaller technology firms though business start-up. The incubators are akin to continuing education facilities that train entrepreneurs in various types of technology. One new example is the Lewis Incubator for Technology (LIFT), which was created in partnership with the National Aeronautics and Space Administration's (NASA) Lewis Research Center in Cleveland. Its purpose is to support those companies that aim to commercialize NASA technologies. According to Department of Development numbers, 130 new companies have "graduated" from Edison Incubators since 1992. The department's estimate on the number of new jobs created via incubation is more than 1,800.

Another Edison offshoot is the Edison Technology Transfer Program, which in essence pairs researchers from private and public sectors on projects. More than fifty cooperative research agreements between industry and federal research giants Wright Patterson Air Force Base and NASA Lewis have been forged since 1992. The costs of the research, however, are not a 50–50 split. The state of Ohio has paid about $6 million, Uncle Sam about $13 million. Governor Voinovich also sought to increase recognition for the companies that were taking leadership roles not just in use of technology for their own ends but in improving the quality of life for the world. The Edison Award was first presented in 1993 to Cincinnati-based Procter & Gamble. Starting in 1995 five to seven Emerging Technology Awards were given annually to smaller companies that had demonstrated success on a smaller scale.

One partnership in promoting technology apart from the Edison Program was launched in November 1997. ConnectOhio, a partnership between Ameritech and the Department of Development, is a web-site repository of information. Chief of its several purposes is the promotion of electronic commerce and the connection of businesses with related state resources.

Ohio efforts to clean its high-sulfur coal do not appear in daily headlines but have nonetheless won awards in the past eight years. The Ohio Coal Development Office in the Technology Division has shifted its emphasis from research, which marks the beginning of the process to deploy technology, to demonstrations and pilot projects farther along the deployment spectrum. Most of these demonstrations show the benefits of new clean coal technologies (CCTs). Though the original intent of CCT research was to protect Ohio jobs in coal mines and power plants, the goals have evolved to include promoting commercial applications of the processes, as CCTs also produce resaleable by-products that have construction and agricultural uses.

In order to deflect the economic woes that followed reductions in the federal defense budget, Jobs Bill II made provision in 1994 for the Ohio Defense Adjustment Office (ODAO). Grants to affected communities, businesses, and workers totaled $15 million in fiscal years

1995–98. ODAO also advised communities how to reuse defense facilities and how to apply for federal money. ODAO estimates its community efforts helped create or retain more than 7,000 jobs, according to Development documents.

Though training can arguably be categorized as education, some of the training efforts in the Department of Development, as well as its partnership training programs with other state agencies, are aimed precisely at particular jobs and not broadly at imparting general knowledge. One example, the Ohio Industrial Training Program (OITP), provides funds to support customized job-training projects at companies that create or retain jobs. OITP is operated in partnership with the Board of Regents, Department of Education, Bureau of Employment Services, and Department of Human Services. OITP has also entered into a partnership with the federal Appalachian Regional Commission (ARC). For training projects that do not meet OITP qualifications but are located in one of Ohio's twenty-nine Appalachian counties, Funds for Appalachian Retraining (FAIR) has brought in more than $1 million to create or retain more than 1,000 jobs. Despite all the partnering to fund worthwhile economic development projects, some in the twenty-nine Appalachian counties still did not fit guidelines of the ARC and other granting agencies. To remedy these exclusions, Development uses General Revenue Fund money in the form of Mini Grants to pay for such job-generating activities as tourism advertising, research, and conferences.

BUREAU OF EMPLOYMENT SERVICES (OBES)

Simply put, OBES is the jobs department for the state. As such, it has been at the forefront or in partnership with other agencies in all the state's efforts to match job-seekers with employers. One effort of OBES to improve the workplace will be mentioned first because it gets so little mention elsewhere. Governor Voinovich himself requested that OBES implement national skills standards, particularly in metalworking. (The welders' certifications discussed earlier are an example of the impetus to develop valid and reliable standards to certify levels of competency.) Ohio has amassed a list of firsts in the area of national skills standards: (1) Ohio was the first state to become a formal partner in setting standards in two fields, metalworking and printing. (2) Ohio was the first state to implement national skills standards in two fields, machining and metal-stamping. (3) Ohio was the first state to certify workers using new standards. (4) Ohio was the first state to have an official representative on the National Skills Standards Board. (5) Ohio was the first state to create an industry-led skills standards advisory committee at the state level.

It was also OBES's lot, however, to grapple with an irony of the employment scene at the end of the Voinovich administration, both in Ohio and the nation. The unemployment crisis in 1991 metamorphosed into labor shortages in the governor's second term in those businesses dependent on a workforce skilled in technology. True, manufacturing jobs had been lost irretrievably and, yes, new jobs had emerged later in the decade in numbers unimaginable in 1991. But the nature of the work itself had changed. One widely publicized survey of central Ohio business executives by Deloitte & Touche in July 1998 pinpointed a shortage of workers trained in computer science as the number one economic concern from 1998 till the year 2005. Ohio's Senator John Glenn cited computer skills as the chief difference between younger astronauts and himself as he retooled for space travel in October 1998. How OBES has responded to workforce development is a story in process, the plot shifts of which are sometimes explained by the federal government's responses to the same concerns—similar to Governor Voinovich's welfare reform story. To sum up, Ohio floated new ideas, of which the federal government borrowed portions and sent the whole thing back to the states, whereupon Ohio is making adjustments to its course in midjob, so to speak.

The story begins in October 1992, when Governor Voinovich cut the ribbon for the first OBES Customer Services Center in Tiffin. Nicknamed "one-stop," the center's purpose was to coordinate the state's many and various job-training and employment programs in one location. Among the job-training entities represented were OBES job training, the Department of Human Services, adult education, and higher education. The one-stop was a supermarket of job-training options. Another example of consolidation within these pages is the Department of Commerce Regional Customer Service Centers for one-stop licensing and contracting of construction projects. The concept of consolidating similar functions is more than just a convenience for the end-user. The potential for duplication and isolated independence of separated parts of the whole appear time and time again as problems cited by the Operations Improvement Task Force and QStP teams. The one-stop concept, then, was Governor Voinovich's solution to the myriad and far-flung job-training activities conducted by the state on behalf of workers beyond high school.

It was also no mere symbol that standing by the governor's side when he cut the first ribbon at a one-stop was U.S. Secretary of Labor Lynn Martin, who got a firsthand look at the Ohio model. By 1995 federal grant money enabled Ohio to tinker with technological delivery of one-stop services. The one-stops were renamed Employment and Training Centers. Also fully integrated into the one-stop system was Ohio Job Net, a database of job listings and job seekers. What was new about Job Net besides its technological delivery method was the wording of its entries. Instead of mere job openings, listings now detail the skills required to do a job. Likewise, job-seekers record skills they have performed and not just prior job titles. Ohio Job Net's more precise descriptors have led to more referrals for job-seekers—355,000 in 1997, 102,173 of whom moved to new jobs or moved out of the unemployment line. Figures for 1998 up to September show 462,000 referrals via Job Net, resulting in 140,677 placements. The available job openings, though, continue to shrink. In late 1998 the unemployment rate in Ohio hovered around 4 percent, at the lowest sustained level in twenty-five years. Given that about five and a half million Ohioans are working, Job Net clearly is being used by people already employed, who may be seeking advancement or changes, as well as by unemployed people.

By utilizing technology, the number of one-stops has grown from seven regional OBES one-stop offices to 190 separate locations that include a wide range of state and local agencies. While OBES is the lead state agency in the one-stop program, the initiative has evolved into partnerships with five other state agencies—Human Services, Aging, Board of Regents, Education, and Development—and with a host of local partners such as elected officials, business leaders, representatives from organized labor, educators, and various county government agencies.

Governor Voinovich put a mechanism in place in May 1997 that would keep Ohio poised for further changes in workforce development. Created via executive order, the Governor's Workforce Development Board (GWDB) was charged with inspecting the job-training scene "to maximize consistency" in workforce development. Relevant programs included the one-stops already described, the School-to-Work initiative, the Employment Service program, Ohio Works First, Adult Basic and Literacy Education, Carl D. Perkins Vocational and Applied Technology Education, Food Stamp Employment and Training program, the Ohio Industrial Training Program, the Job Training Partnership programs administered by OBES, and any others that might be designated later. A summary of the three recommendations made by the GWDB follows: (1) Find a funding source for the one-stops. At this writing there is no federal or state legislation naming an appropriation for the one-stops. More pressing, federal grants sustaining the one-stops will soon expire. (2) Find a funding source for the School-to-Work initiative, for the same reasons. (3) The GWDB long-term recommendation, a cabinet-level position that vests one person with overall responsibility for workforce development, will be the call of Ohio's next governor.

Governor Voinovich had praised OBES as early as 1993 for its progress in booting up workforce development. "Another key jobs component is workforce training, and I'm very proud of what our

Ohio Bureau of Employment Services accomplished in 1992. At the top of the list is our Workforce Development initiative, which coordinates our thirty-one workforce programs in fifteen separate agencies and gives them, for the first time, a clear strategic focus and common mission."

The School-to-Work (STW) initiative, which is the workforce development program for future workers, is an umbrella covering programs in career exploration and preparedness. Some of the methods are time-tested, some are new and experimental—geared to a workplace that is changing too fast to rely solely on instruction that may be outmoded before the pertinent textbooks are printed and distributed. STW lets students try on a job for fit while they are still in school to make adjustments. It also lets businesses evangelize for certain job skills, in hopes that schools will adjust their coursework and preparation to fit job opportunities. But there are more parties involved in STW than the potential employee and eventual employer in an apprentice-style one-on-one relationship. STW pivots on partnerships at the local level: schools that will permit students to leave the classroom to test what they are learning, businesses that will let students sample actual tasks, labor unions that keep the schools current on actual skills in real jobs, parents who endorse the concept, and community organizations like scout councils that see their stake and respond with opportunities that coordinate with the other STW groups. The idea originated in 1994 federal legislation. In 1996 Ohio launched its own School-to-Work office under the aegis of Lieutenant Governor Nancy Hollister. Five state agencies collaborate to guide the local expressions of job exploration for future workers: OBES, Department of Development, Department of Education, Department of Human Services, and the Ohio Board of Regents. To strike the best balance between opportunities and distances in developing local collaborations, the state was divided into twelve STW regions.

The level of exposure students choose to a particular career ranges from a field trip to pairing with a mentor in the field to an internship for a semester to the extended relationships of apprenticeships and co-op programs, a term that usually describes a half-school/half-work experience across more than one year. In addition to those traditional configurations are innovations that fit the times. For example, Total Quality Management—the workplace problem-solving concept that operates in Ohio state government as QStP—has made its way into the high school at Belpre, where students, city officials, chamber of commerce staffers, and Shell Chemical employees all work in teams to solve real problems. A semester course on team-style learning is planned for the school curriculum in Belpre for the 1998–99 school year. Furthermore, the very notion of career study, the longtime purview of high school juniors and seniors, is being extended to lower grades. One example is a project in Conesville Elementary School aimed to bolster science skills for grade schoolers. In symbiosis with the area Labor-Management Cooperative Council of East Central Ohio, youngsters apply classroom assignments to a wetlands project, a learn-by-doing exercise that also integrates applications to the work world.

The governor reinforced his dedication to the new programs that bridge school and the workplace and that provide ongoing training for adults in the 1996 State of the State Address. "The only states that will prosper in the 21st century are those committed to lifelong learning. There are far too many people today in America who are anxious about the future because of the tremendous changes, driven by technology, that are taking place in the workforce. Our commitment to lifelong learning can help those people find a place in the high-performance workplace of today and tomorrow."

"The only states that will prosper in the 21st century are those committed to lifelong learning."

DEPARTMENT OF REHABILITATION AND CORRECTION

Ohio Penal Industries (OPI) are shops within the state's correctional institutes that function not only to keep inmates occupied, but also to teach work ethics and specific skills that may help the inmates get and keep a job after release. During the Voinovich administration, the number of institutions with OPI shops increased from sixteen to twenty-one. The overall number of shops also grew, from thirty-five to fifty-five. Growth was largest in the number of private sector shops within institutions, from two to fifteen. New types of training were also added to boost the chances of inmate employability after incarceration—in drafting, computer graphics, computer testing and repair, mulch and composting, construction operations, tele-marketing, copier repair, and laser cartridge refurbishing. In addition to new training, the department worked harder to help inmates on the verge of release in their pursuit of jobs. In a program supported by Governor Voinovich called Job Linkage, the department hosted twenty-one job fairs in 1997 for employers to interview 804 inmates. Though outright job offers cannot be extended until after an inmate leaves prison, more than half the interviewees at the job fairs were asked to contact the person who had interviewed them. The department also hosted three seminars in 1997 for those employers interested in hiring released inmates.

Soon after he took office in 1991 Governor Voinovich urged prison officials to come up with community service activities for inmates. Some of the work performed by inmates was refurbishing computers for schools, helping the Department of Transportation remove roadside litter and weeds, rehabbing houses for low- and moderate-income families, and raising and training pilot dogs for blind people. The time spent by inmates on such community work increased from 50,000 hours in 1991 to 2.5 million hours in 1997, according to figures from the Department of Rehabilitation and Correction.

One cost-cutting law that took effect in March 1998 may have had a serendipitous effect on the number of work hours recorded by prison inmates. Prisoners who visit a doctor are now required to co-pay $3.00 of the cost of a nonemergency visit, these co-payments being drawn from inmates' accounts. The cost-cutting motive yielded $89,500 in only five months, to be applied to medical care costs for prisons. The by-product was a reduction in the number of inmates who skipped work. The daily sick call dropped from 626 before Senate Bill 111 to an average of 345 per day in August, according to department tallies.

DEPARTMENT OF TAXATION

Beginning in 1993, the Department of Taxation played a part in economic development by teaching the details of business taxes in Small Business Workshops, presented jointly with the Internal Revenue Service in locations throughout the state. Workshop participants receive workbooks and a business tax kit with all the forms and publications a business will need to file taxes. Summary data from the department puts the total number of workshops held since 1993 at 177 and the number of small businesses represented at 4,857. For those companies that merely want updating, the department sponsors the annual Ohio Tax Conference in collaboration with the Ohio Chamber of Commerce. For twenty years the conference has focused on changes in tax law and policy for both business and state and local governments. In the past two years, however, Taxa-

"We gave Ohio's economic engine a long overdue tune-up."

tion has polished its offerings to attract more participants from more places outside Ohio. At the 1998 conference, representatives of corporations, law firms, accounting firms and state and local governments totaled 475, up from 405 at the 1997 conference.

The governor himself summarized all these efforts in his last State of the State Address in 1998. "Together we committed ourselves to achieving our Ohio 2000/Ohio First vision of strengthening Ohio's place as a national leader and world-class competitor, both now and into the 21st century. We focused on Ohio's strengths—agribusiness, travel and tourism, science and technology, and international trade —and we've made significant gains in each area. We gave Ohio's economic engine a long overdue tune-up."

CHAPTER 4

Education

"I am convinced that a world-class education is the best way to help every Ohio citizen make the most of his or her God-given talents. It is also our best economic development tool and the best investment we can make in the future."

PROFESSOR OF PARTNERSHIPS

WITHIN THE FIRST minute of his first Inaugural Address, Governor Voinovich announced one thing he would do immediately for education without lobbying anyone—"Earlier this morning, the Governor's Office adopted Douglas Elementary School." Seated with him on the dais was the champion of the state's Adopt-a-School program, First Lady Janet Voinovich. Thus began his promotion of partnerships between specific schools and a host of businesses, service organizations, and state agencies that would become a litany by the end of the Voinovich era. The process is simple. Personnel from the adopting organizations tutor students, offer career advice, provide in-kind resources appropriate to the match, speak on their professional activities, and participate not only in routine activities, but also in innovative ways agreed upon as part of the relationship.

Governor Voinovich, who said the Adopt-a-School program fit his philosophy of individuals "making a difference in someone's life," urged state agencies to adopt schools. One of the best examples in state government was the Adjutant General's Department, which coaxed nearly ninety National Guard units into the adopter role. In the 1995 Inaugural Address, the governor reported that thirty-four state agencies had adopted schools. "This program has expanded to about one-third of all Ohio school districts and school buildings," he said. "Janet's goal is to see to it that every Ohio school has a partner and every child who needs a mentor, has one." By the 1995–96 school year, there were 388 partnerships throughout Ohio using the Adopt-a-School model that brought 4,000 employees into contact with schools. By late 1998, some Ohio schools had as many as five adopters each, with the total of adopters topping 4,000.

To shape education reform in Ohio, Governor Voinovich applied the same model he had fostered in management and economic development—forging partnerships between government and the private sector. In his first State of the State Address, Governor Voinovich announced that he had selected the forum of the Ohio Business Roundtable to define the parameters of school improvements in Ohio. He established the Governor's Education Management Council (GEM) to conduct an audit of public education in Ohio—examining governance, finances, and the path to improvement on the national education goals. The "Education for Results" reform package that GEM recommended was founded on the twin pillars of casting improvements in terms that could be reliably measured and making school relevant to the workplace. In addition the governor supported the participation of BEST (an acronym for Building Excellent Schools for Today and the 21st Century), a coalition of more than a hundred business, community, education, and parent organizations that led the way into school involvement. Partnerships, particularly with business, continued to be the rule in one initiative after another in the governor's quest for school reform. As he said in his second Inaugural Address, "Show me a school district where the local business community is involved, and I'll show you a school district that's improving."

That school reform is necessary was not refuted in the 1990s. Serious efforts to improve schools had begun in 1983 after the release of *A Nation at Risk,* the often cited report of the National Commission on Excellence in Education that warned of "a rising tide of mediocrity" in American schools. To some, though, school reform meant only to reform the money; i.e., spend more. To others it meant only to reform the academics; i.e., demand performance at a higher standard. To Governor Voinovich it meant "education results—results that will be demanded, measured, and rewarded," as he said in the 1993 State of the State Address. However, the new fiscal commitments by the state deserve a review before recapping the efforts to experiment with innovations in academics. Education, after all, is an exception to the Voinovich watchword of "do more with less." In the 1991 speech that announced his plans to reform education, he announced in the next breath: "I am also committed to increasing education's share of the state budget. To that end, in spite of our financial crisis, there will be no cuts in the first fiscal year in basic aid, a 5 percent increase in the second year, and a $50 million equity fund." But that infusion would have an accounting. As he said later in the speech, "We've got to set standards. We have to tell Ohio's employers that our high school graduates at least have ninth grade reading, writing and mathematics skills and a basic understanding of citizenship."

A discussion of school reform cannot proceed without mentioning the hurdles of varying height set up around this track. One governor can adopt a school, but thousands of people have a say in education reform. Few real changes can commence without legislative concurrence. Another variable is the structure of the education hierarchy itself. From the beginning of his first term, Governor Voinovich had lobbied for changes in Ohio's governance of public education. The legislature concurred with him and reduced the number of elected members on the Board of Education to eleven, then gave the governor authority to appoint eight members. The board selects the Superintendent of Public Instruction. Add to that the fact that individual school districts in turn are governed by elected school boards whose task includes negotiations with teacher unions. A new player entered the arena in the 1990s when the courts ruled against the adequacy of Ohio's funding methods for public schools. Rather than recite the complete history of the DeRolph case, suffice it to say that any questions about school funding reform are still questions. Last, as in the case of the May 1998 sales tax vote and dozens of local referenda on levy increases yearly, voters occasionally weigh in. These are the realities that challenge those who would chalk up changes in schools.

REFURBISHING BUDGETS, EQUITY, AND BUILDINGS

Governor Voinovich began to tackle the behemoth of school finance reform in his first year in office. Despite court deliberations that leave the issue hanging in the balance at this writing, and despite the voters' rejection of a proposed sales tax increase, progress was clearly made on his pledge to increase spending on education. Summaries read this way: Between FY 1991 and FY 1999 General Revenue Fund items for education, including state property tax reimbursement to school districts, will increase $2 billion, or 50.7 percent. Because the inflation rate for the period is estimated at 25.9 percent, the increase is significant, according to figures from the Office of Budget and Management. The usual measure for judging adequacy of school spending is the Basic Aid per pupil foundation level. The amount has grown between FY 1991 and FY 1999 from $2,636 to $3,851, or 46 percent above FY 1991 with an inflation rate of 25.9 percent for those years. When state, local, and federal sources of revenue are combined, the figure available to all school districts (as of FY 1997) is more than $4,000 per pupil.

Local sources of revenue, however, create disparities. Ohio is not the only state to deal with the inequities engendered by a reliance on local property taxes to subsidize schools. As the governor said in his 1991 State of the State Address, "The current formula has helped create rich and poor school districts. The Ohio Public Expenditure Council recently pointed out that the per pupil allocation ranges from $3,000 to $11,000 per student." To reduce the polarity in that range of numbers, Governor Voinovich proposed an equity fund in his first budget. In FY 1993 the first resources flowed into the fund and have been increased each year since. The fund is intended to provide extra dollars, above basic aid, to the 292 lowest-wealth school districts of the 611 school districts in the state. The $591 million distributed to poorer school districts through FY 1998 translates into a 56.5 percent increase in per-pupil expenditure since 1991 for the poorest one-fourth of Ohio's schools.

Other techniques were implemented to equalize the amount school districts got from the state. The amount of locally contributed money used to calculate the state's funding support was increased to 23 mils from 20 mils by 1997. The introduction of an ability-to-pay factor separate from property values was integrated into the computation in 1996. The reasons for the leveling were made clear by Governor Voinovich in several speeches, but the clearest expression was in the 1995 State of the State Address: "I am convinced that a world-class education is the best way to help every Ohio citizen make the most of his or her God-given talents. It is also our best economic development tool and the best investment we can make in the future."

A flurry of changes in school financing appeared in House Bill 650, enacted as a response to the Ohio Supreme Court's *DeRolph* ruling of 1998. At the request of the governor, the legislature revisited school financing in 1998 and adopted much of what had been recommended by the Voinovich School Reform Task Force in 1997 (which is also referred to as the Augenblick formula). In fact, the task force's work had been praised by experts and passed by the Ohio Senate, but died in the House before its partial resurrection in 1998.

What did emerge in House Bill 650 was a "rational based foundation level" formula for determining how much state money a school district gets. The legislature reviewed the costs of the most successful school districts in Ohio to derive a per-pupil foundation level of $4,063. Eliminated was "categorical unit funding" in comprehensive high schools, which was the mechanism for deciding how much state money a school district would get for the "units" of special and vocational education. Students needing those services will be weighted and included as part of their district's attendance in the foundation calculation. Additional attempts to insure fairness in calculating the Basic Aid amount will incorporate such variables as districts' special education costs, number of pupils receiving public assistance, cost-of-doing-business, transportation costs, equalizations for low property values, and chargeoff supplements to protect districts from major losses when property taxes are rolled back. Preliminary estimates from OBM on the effects of the new formulas predict that funding for education will increase more than 40 percent over 1998 levels by FY 2003, or 2.5 times the current rate of inflation.

Elsewhere in the state's role as leavening agent for school spending, attention was paid to the school buildings themselves, for everyone involved in education was aware of the age and deterioration of schools in low-wealth districts, long before the airing of nationally syndicated documentaries on the subject. Indeed, the governor's widely announced education platform had underscored the need to use state resources to rebuild Ohio's crumbling schools. Thus in 1993 the Voinovich administration put forth dollar-amount recommendations for capital improvements in schools—in unprecedented amounts. The combination of cash and debt-supported funds made available for school renovations and construction from FY 1992 to FY 1998 totals $1.06 billion, from both Operating and Capital Budget acts, according to data from the Office of Budget and Management. In fact, a separate entity was created at the governor's insistence just to focus on assisting schools with building needs. Called the Ohio School Facilities Commission, the three-member group consists of the Superintendent of Public Instruction, the Director of Administrative Services, and the Director of Budget and Management.

In the past, state assistance for facilities was not only smaller, but also distributed in no discernible pattern. The legislature resolved the prioritization matter of who would get funds when by carving the state's school districts into tiers based on wealth, each tier composed of 5 percent of all districts, with allocation priority determined by a combination of wealth level and need. Allocations to those districts most in need within the tier were agreed upon before moving on to the next tier. Districts themselves are still responsible for some part of the costs of renovation or new construction and for all of the subsequent maintenance and upkeep. But as some of the districts have found, a commitment that the state will pay the majority of the costs for a new school is an incentive for voters to pass new tax levies. Other special considerations were covered in the facilities assistance plan: $100 million in matching funds was provided for urban schools for major repairs and renovations, and $130 million was made available for low-wealth schools needing emergency repairs.

In addition, the capital appropriations bill proposed by Governor Voinovich in November 1998 would add $505 million to funds for primary and secondary school buildings. Passed by the legislature in December 1998, the amount brings the total of state funding support provided for school building assistance since 1993 to more than $1.56 billion.

TESTING STEWARDSHIP PROFICIENCY

The state of Ohio did not allocate more money without first setting in place some mechanisms to ensure it was spent appropriately. Several accountability measures went into effect during the Voinovich years:

1. State audits of districts with fiscal problems so severe that reductions in force may ensue

2. Creation of a solvency fund to keep districts from fiscal disaster when emergencies occur

3. Elimination of district borrowing against projected property tax receipts beginning in 1999

4. Cessation of emergency loans after March 1, 1998

5. Establishment of school district budget reserve funds of 5 percent of the district budget—on the pattern of the state's Rainy Day Fund

6. Submission by districts of five-year budget plans to the state

7. Designation of 4 percent of the district budget into two funds each—one for buildings and maintenance, the other for textbooks and materials

8. Certification that the district does indeed have the resources to provide an adequate educational program

Perhaps the most visible of the accountability actions was the publication of School Report Cards for each district and for the state as a whole based not only on fiscal management but also on academic achievement. The Department of Education even devised a few proficiency categories for the schools to pass muster on—eighteen to be exact—and a grading system that ranged from "effective" to "in a state of academic emergency." In his last State of the State Address in 1998, Governor Voinovich predicted that the School Report Cards and other accountability measures would result in "the most significant improvement in classroom performance in Ohio history. That's because, at long last, our customers—the parents and taxpayers—will know what they're getting for their investment."

NETTING RESULTS IN TECHNOLOGY

On another spending front, this one decidedly specific, Governor Voinovich launched a program to put computer technology literally within the reach of every child in an Ohio public school. As he said in the 1994 State of the State Address:

I am today announcing SchoolNet, Ohio's commitment to bring telecommunications and computer technology into the classroom over the next five years. SchoolNet has three primary components. The first step is to wire every classroom in every school to provide for voice, video, and data transmission, including interactive distance learning. I am suggesting that $50 million in the upcoming capital budget be set aside to fund this initiative, beginning with our lowest-wealth districts. Second, another $45 million in capital funding will be earmarked to put a computer with CD-ROM capability and a modem, or other related equipment, in every classroom in the poorest 25 percent of the public school districts, an estimated 14,000 classrooms. Third, we must make a greater state investment to help provide in-service training for our teachers, to make sure they are prepared to utilize this technology and take advantage of other break-the-mold concepts that will move Ohio ahead of the class.

He then cited the advantages of SchoolNet: to expand curriculum, to give students access to the best experts and teachers through cyberspace, to network schools with libraries, and to provide the most up-to-date information. SchoolNet was authorized by the legislature that year at $95 million—$45 million for computers, $50 million for wiring—in low-wealth school districts. As of July 1998, 83 percent of the eligible classrooms were wired or in process. The latest projection for completion of the wiring of all eligible classrooms is December 1999.

The year after SchoolNet was announced, the governor and legislature upped state spending for computers with SchoolNet Plus, the goal of which was to place one computer workstation for every five children in grades kindergarten through four in public schools. By late 1997, $400 million had been committed to 99 percent of the eligible K–4 classrooms in Ohio. To support further the computerization of Ohio's classrooms, the state earmarked $30 million from FY 1997 lottery profits for electrical upgrades in older buildings. Also in the list of state expenditures to upgrade technology in schools was $48 million for teacher training in applying the latest hardware and software to classroom instruction. The total appropriation for SchoolNet and SchoolNet Plus reached $526.7 million by FY 1999.

The governor also saw to it that the capability for distance learning was brought to schools at no cost or very low cost. Working through the Public Utilities Commission of Ohio, Governor Voinovich tied telephone company regulation to commitments by phone companies to provide networking and assistance to schools. The PUCO chairman also serves as a member of the Information, Learning, and Technology Authority.

In a related upgrade of computer capability that benefits schools, Governor Voinovich recommended and got passage of legislation establishing the Ohio Public Library Information Network (OPLIN) in 1996. Though the name clarifies OPLIN's function to connect all the libraries in the state, it does not reveal that schools are connected, too. From a keyboard in a classroom miles away from a university or urban library, students and teachers can tap databases that would take days or weeks to get via interlibrary loan. The governor called it

"An access ramp to the information superhighway"

"an access ramp to the information superhighway" when he announced it in 1995. OPLIN also reduces libraries' costs while it reduces patrons' time spent on researching. Among the types of information available via OPLIN are electronic card catalogs, news, weather, and reference data.

COMPETITION COMES TO SCHOOL— VENTURES, VOUCHERS, AND VARIATIONS

The governor's Venture Capital idea bridges the separate categories of finance and academics in public schools, for the program gives new money to schools, but money based on a convincing grant application focused on academics instead of sheer need. Grants in the amount of $25,000 per year for five years were awarded to 600 schools that made a case for trying something different that fit their locales. The new tack might be a program to increase parental involvement, or to increase attendance, to name two examples from an array of options. Stipulations are that the grantee school must specify its plans to develop a research-based idea, test it, and implement it. Total spent by the end of 1997 in Venture Capital outlays was $56 million, according to Governor's Office data.

Innovative programs designed and championed by local districts are one way to introduce change to schools. Standing back and suggesting innovations to the entire system, though, may make an establishment edgy, as the governor found out when he suggested school choice in the 1995 State of the State Address. "Another initiative I want to place on Ohio's smorgasbord of education reform is a pilot school scholarship plan. I want Ohio to be the first state to have an honest-to-goodness experiment in school choice. How will we know if it works or not if we don't at least try it?"

Based on the premise that competition fosters improvement, Governor Voinovich's choice plan introduced another v-word to Ohio— voucher. Anathema to public schools, which do not benefit from their use, vouchers are publicly financed scholarships that make private schools, including religious schools, affordable for people who couldn't otherwise afford the tuition payments. Eligible to apply in Ohio are parents with low incomes whose children will be in kindergarten through fourth grades in Cleveland Public Schools. The parents must contribute 10 to 25 percent (depending on income) of the voucher, the maximum value of which is $2,500. Key to understanding the opposition is the simple reminder that public education is still a monopoly just as surely as public utilities used to be. The plan is under challenge in state courts. In the 1996 State of the State Address, the governor said, "And for the life of me, I cannot understand why the education lobby is fighting our scholarship program in the Cleveland Public Schools, which gives 1,500 low-income families real choices in deciding where to send their children to school. To those who would stand in the way, I say: 'Give those parents a choice.'" In its third year, with 4,000 participants in 56 schools, parents reported high satisfaction and students logged higher achievement scores, according to data and surveys from the state.

Regardless of the outcome on vouchers in the courts, states do provide aid to non-public schools. (Aid *per se* to non-public schools was approved by the U.S. Supreme Court in 1977.) Designed for purchases of equipment and materials, the goal is to standardize curriculum and administration, which could make measurements between private and public schools more meaningful. Under Governor Voinovich, Ohio now leads the nation in state support of non-public schools, which educate one in seven of Ohio's children.

Also put on the smorgasbord in 1997 was an idea to experiment with the administrative structure of public schools. Charter schools, or community schools as they are sometimes called in Ohio, are independent of any public school district and exempt from certain state statutes and rules. Any public school in the state can become a community school. In addition, new community schools can be created in any of Ohio's eight largest school districts. The schools must specify their objectives and commit to annual progress reports and evaluations based on how well they meet their academic goals. Not meeting contract obligations or goals could result in charter revocation. In 1997 Governor Voinovich and the General Assembly agreed to a five-year pilot program in Lucas County complete with state grant money. Because an exodus of students from non-charter schools would reduce the state Basic Aid allocation to a district, the home districts will receive half the allocation for each student who chooses to attend a charter school in that district.

Another opportunity for trial-and-error began in 1997. Deregulation was initiated in eleven school districts in a pilot program structurally midway between Venture Capital grants, which permit the testing of a specific idea within a district, and charter school contracts, which permit changing virtually everything. In short, the deregulated schools got temporary waivers from rules and regulations (both state and federal) in order to implement research on new governance or teaching methods. The participating districts, limited at first to those with high academic scores, share a pool of $2 million to be spent on research and development of innovations, but not on personnel or infrastructure. The dependent variable is of course student academic achievement. By early 1997, 143 waivers had been granted, with 123 of those geared to experiment with the school calendar so that teachers could take advantage of professional development opportunities.

The state's new Open Enrollment law, like the voucher experiment, is predicated on the simple premise that parents will choose the school they perceive to be best for their children if given the choice. But this choice is different because it removes private schools from the picture altogether in the competition for students. It requires the state's public schools to establish policies on crossing the lines that define geographic districts. Parents could send their children to different schools, whether intradistrict to another neighborhood or interdistrict to an adjacent district, if the school districts choose to participate. In Voinovich fashion, the adjacent districts form *de facto* partnerships about the procedures of student exchanges. In the latest addition to Open Enrollment law, parents could travel even farther from home in search of the right school for their children and select a district that is not even adjacent to their home one, if the school districts choose to participate. As might be expected, certain limits to open enrollment apply: capacity of the building, grade, or program; preferences for students who do live within district lines; and assurance that racial balances will be maintained.

URBAN SCHOOLS INITIATIVE

The governor was particularly concerned about changing the conditions in Ohio's urban schools. In 1996 he cited these statistics: "It has been said about the Cleveland Public Schools that, barring a dramatic turnaround, fifty of every hundred of today's eighth graders will drop out of school. Only thirty-three will graduate from high school, and fewer than ten of these will have passed the twelfth-grade proficiency test. And the numbers in Ohio's other urban districts are not encouraging." He went on to repeat the figures that have held for decades: three-fourths of the people on welfare and in prison are high school dropouts. The Urban Schools Initiative (USI), which was developed by the governor and the Ohio Board of Education in 1997, featured changes in eight areas:

1. All-day kindergarten to improve academic performance in the long run

2. School Readiness Resource Centers, three per district in twenty-one urban areas, which link schools with the social services provided under the Ohio Family and Children First Council

3. Jobs for Ohio's Graduates, a school-to-work outreach program promoted for at-risk high school students

4. Discipline Intervention Grants to head off dropping out and to increase attendance

5. Urban Leadership Academies to enable teachers and principals in the six largest urban districts of Ohio to focus on instructional challenges pertinent to their situations

6. Professional development via a peer review process, complete with mentors and assessors for beginning teachers

7. Performance audits with Urban Initiative funding contingent on districts' addressing recommendations of the audits

8. Academic benchmarks, as of May 1998, for twenty-one urban districts that will be compared to future measures on such issues as graduation and attendance rates, dropout numbers, and proficiency test scores

(The title of the complete report by the USI in 1997 is *Through the Eyes of a Child.*) The governor continued his commitment to the Urban Initiative despite criticism from some who thought he was spending too much. He responded in 1997: "Ohio's greatest resource is our peo-

"Ohio's greatest resource is our people."

ple, and thousands of our young people from those urban districts are not fully developing their God-given talents. I believe it is our moral responsibility to respond."

"EDUCATION IS EVERYBODY'S BUSINESS"

Other efforts in the realm of education during the Voinovich gubernatorial terms stemmed from the list of national goals in education endorsed by former President George Bush and the nation's governors in 1989. By 1994, the goals had been incorporated into federal law (Goals 2000: Educate America Act), with two more added to the original six. The reader may be steeped in the goals, vaguely familiar with them, or unaware of them altogether. Because they serve as the strategic framework for the governor's efforts to improve much of what was happening in Ohio under the rubric of education, they are listed below.

Goal #1: By the year 2000, all children in America will start school ready to learn.

Goal #2: By the year 2000, the high school graduation rate will increase to at least 90 percent.

Goal #3: By the year 2000, American students will leave grades four, eight, and twelve having demonstrated competency in challenging subject matter including English, mathematics, science, foreign languages, civics and government, economics, arts, history, and geography; and every school in America will ensure that all students learn to use their minds well, so they may be prepared for responsible citizenship, further learning, and productive employment in our modern economy.

Goal #4: By the year 2000, the nation's teaching force will have access to programs for the continued improvement of their professional skills and the opportunity to acquire the knowledge and skills needed to instruct and prepare all American students for the next century.

Goal #5: By the year 2000, U.S. students will be the first in the world in mathematics and science achievement.

Goal #6: By the year 2000, every adult American will be literate and will possess the knowledge and skills necessary to compete in a global economy and to exercise the rights and responsibilities of citizenship.

Goal #7: By the year 2000, every school in the United States will be free of drugs, violence, and the unauthorized presence of firearms and alcohol, and will offer a disciplined environment conducive to learning.

Goal #8: By the year 2000, every school will promote partnerships that will increase parental involvement and participation in promoting the social, emotional and academic growth of children.

"Education is everybody's business," Governor Voinovich said in his first Inaugural Address. The goals underscore that point, because four of them (#1, #4, #6, and #8) are out of the control of kindergarten-through-twelfth-grade schools altogether, while #7 adds a policing function to schools that was not imaginable a generation ago. Achieving those three that are within the traditional job descriptions of schools (#2, #3, and #5) requires changing traditional ways of doing things. The governor said in his first State of the State Address in 1991 that he was committed to the goals. Then the next year he announced, "At the request of the National Governors' Association, I have taken a national leadership role with respect to the goals, heading up school readiness, one of three national action teams."

GOAL #1—SCHOOL READINESS

Head Start

Governor Voinovich made a pledge in the 1991 State of the State Address that became one of his personal goals, a promise on which he would mark progress in subsequent speeches. Renouncing government's role in perpetuating a cycle of welfare, poverty, drugs, and crime, he said the only way to free the people trapped within the cycle "is to pick one generation of children, draw a line in the sand, and say to all: 'This is where it stops.' Today we draw that line." Then he revealed that in spite of the budgetary abyss, "nearly all programs in our budget affecting children have either been protected or expanded." Specifically, he said he would increase the number of children enrolled in Head Start, the preschool program begun in 1965 as part of then-President Lyndon B. Johnson's Great Society. Open to low-income youngsters aged three and four, Head Start aims to ready "the whole child" for school by ensuring proper nutrition, hygiene, and parental involvement in activities that address the academic, physical, emotional, and social needs of children.

Ohio is now the national leader in state support for Head Start, spending $181.3 million in FY 1998 compared to $18.4 million in 1990, according to Governor's Office figures. Ohio is also the national leader in percentage of eligible children served—90 percent—while nationally the percentage served is 40 percent, according to figures from the National Head Start Association. When Head Start is combined with other early education programs, all children at or below 100 percent of the poverty level in Ohio who want preschool services have access to them. The goal, of course, is for 100 percent of Ohio's eligible children to move from access to actual enrollment. Ohio is almost there. The percentage of children in Head Start and other preschool offerings reached 87 percent in 1998. When percentages are translated to numbers of children, the comparisons are 66,000 preschoolers enrolled in FY 1999, up from 6,300 children in 1991 in combined preschool programs.

Ohio Family and Children First

"I am committed to doing everything in my power to assure that every Ohio child is healthy and prepared, not just for school, but for life itself," Governor Voinovich said in 1991. Acting on his belief that "education begins at conception," he proposed the Ohio Family and Children First Initiative (OFCF) in 1992 to reach children in order to prepare them for school and life. In early 1994 he reported on the nine OFCF pilot projects, "which are helping us find local, home-grown solutions to cut government red tape, coordinate service delivery, and assure that the dollars we spend on our families are being spent wisely." Though the overall goal of Family and Children First is to help children enter school ready to learn, the program has three specific objectives: (1) assuring that infants are healthier, (2) increasing access to quality preschool and child care for families desiring enrollment, and (3) improving services to aid family stability. Two of those goals are clearly quality of life issues and will be taken up in Chapter 5, but the goals for early childhood education belong in a discussion of Ohio's efforts to achieve Goal #1 on the national list.

"I am committed to doing everything in my power to assure that every Ohio child is healthy and prepared, not just for school, but for life itself."

More than a dozen separate efforts in early childhood services provided by the state have been coordinated under the Ohio Family and Children First umbrella. In addition to Head Start, there are HeadStart/Child Care Partnerships that offer all-day, year-round care for young children. Numbers from a Governor's Office report in 1998 record 5,770 children served in 258 centers linked with Head Start and another 460 children cared for in 242 home settings. More such partnerships are in the planning stage. Using the Head Start standards, Ohio has also revamped both its Public Preschool programs and Preschool Special Education. Numbers of children enrolled in 1997 were 7,655 in Public Preschool and more than 3,000 in Preschool Special Education. In terms of percentages, between 80 and 90 percent of eligible children ages three to five were enrolled in one of these two programs in 1998.

Child care subsidized with state and federal money is another of the preschool efforts. When Governor Voinovich took office, child care spending was $37 million. In FY 1999, the budget for child care is $252 million. The number of children enrolled is another way to see growth in Ohio's child care support. In 1992, about 18,000 children per month benefited from subsidized child care. By 1999 that number will reach 81,000 per month. Child care is also subsidized in Ohio via a set of tax credits for employers who support child care. Whether the assistance is establishment of an on-site center, payments to an off-site licensed center, or reimbursements to the employee, employers can take credits equal to half their various costs, within certain limits, beginning in 1998.

The state also has its own Early Childhood Centers. Four state agencies contribute funding for fifteen centers statewide, with twenty-one more in the works. Abiding by the OFCF precept of forging partnerships for speedy delivery of services, the four state agencies also team up with local agencies to increase access to education and health care services for preschoolers. The departments of Mental Health, Mental Retardation and Developmental Disabilities, Human Services, and Education pioneered the centers in 1998 under the aegis of Ohio Family and Children First. In a closely related improvement, seven state agencies are working toward consolidated licensing functions to speed up the process for licensure of public-use facilities such as the Early Childhood Centers.

Early Start is a home visitation program aimed at preventing child abuse, neglect, or delays in delivery of development services. The state provided flexible funding in 1996 to thirty counties for identification and support of infants and toddlers who might need prevention or early intervention services. The FY 1998 budget expands the program to all eighty-eight Ohio counties using more TANF dollars. Since 1996 more than 7,100 families with infants and toddlers have been visited by Early Start staffers, who answer questions about child development, listen to concerns, or direct families to additional resources. In 1999, Early Start should reach an estimated 25,000 families with children under age three.

"Read two Dr. Seuss books while resting on the sofa" might be an actual prescription written by an Ohio pediatrician in one early childhood program that is a first in Ohio. In a partnership among the Ohio chapters of the American Academy of Pediatrics, Kiwanis International, and the American Library Association, Reach Out and

Read volunteers encourage parents to read to their youngsters in any setting that suits parent and child. Kiwanis members offer to read to kids in physicians' waiting rooms, while libraries help buy books for those who can't afford them. Television is also pressed into service in teaching preschoolers about safety, nutrition, and hygiene. OFCF, along with the Department of Human Services, is working with Ohio Educational Television Services in a program aimed at home-based child care providers. Public television stations will also receive funds to conduct workshops on how to make best use of popular children's shows as teaching tools.

The governor re-emphasized his commitment to education for children age birth to three in the 1998 State of the State Address, "I have made it my top priority. We're doing so because science is teaching us more and more about those crucial first three years of a child's life, when brain capacity grows more than at any other time. We know that an infant's experiences during those years will literally shape the brain's structure and learning capacity for a lifetime." National leaders in early childhood circles are aware of the efforts undertaken in Ohio to achieve Goal #1. Judsen Culbreth, editor-in-chief of *Working Mother* magazine, said of Governor Voinovich, "You are a pioneer for our time. You have led an entire state and the communities throughout the state to collaborate in achieving the First National Education Goal of school readiness for all children. Your example stands as a powerful call to action." The 1997 reports of the Kaufman Foundation and Pew Charitable Trust also praised Ohio's attention to children. Both cited Ohio for doing more than any other state to increase early childhood funding significantly and to demonstrate sustained commitment to long-term reform of its education and human services systems.

GOAL #2—A DIPLOMA IN EVERY HAND

The goal of a 90 percent graduation rate by the year 2000 is reachable in Ohio. When diplomas were handed out in 1998, the high schools in the state had attained an 80 percent graduation rate, with one-third of the high schools already at the 90 percent goal. Though the groundwork is being laid for long-term programs aimed at overcoming the factors that lead to dropping out, the state already has at least five programs in place to help students graduate from high school.

1. Ohio has set aside funds for alternative schools for students with different learning styles or different instructional needs.

2. Under Governor Voinovich, the Jobs for Ohio Graduates (JOG) program has been expanded. Those students deemed at risk of dropping out are encouraged to stay in school, graduate, and make the transition to work, college, or military after graduation under JOG supervision. They are taught not only how to do a particular job, but also how to write a resume, how to interview, and how to apply for a job. Governor Voinovich's success in applying the national Jobs for America's Graduates program to Ohio earned him a national leadership award from JAG in 1993. He was named JAG chairman in 1995. Funded by the state, corporate sponsors, and participating school districts, the Ohio model yielded a graduation rate of 90 percent for the class of 1994 participants. Nine months later 83 percent were employed or continuing their education.

3. The function of the GRADS program is to keep pregnant or parenting teens in school. An acronym for Graduation, Reality, and Dual-Role Skills, the program provides in-school help in setting career goals.

4. Learning, Earning, and Parenting (LEAP) provides financial incentives and sanctions to teen parents to encourage attendance in school or an alternative educational program. LEAP is administered by the Department of Human Services.

5. Under the direction of the Urban Schools Initiative, state grant money is being allocated to help students involved with the juvenile justice system stay in school.

Meanwhile, 98 percent of Ohio's high school graduates had passed all portions of the ninth-grade proficiency tests in reading, writing, mathematics, and citizenship by graduation day 1998. But Governor

Voinovich raised the bar for high school graduation by signing a law to increase the number of credits required and to strengthen state proficiency tests, which a student must pass in order to graduate. The number of Carnegie units required to graduate was increased from 18 to 21, and required courses increased from 9 to 14 by the year 2001. The proficiency tests required for graduation, currently normed for eighth graders, will be replaced by tenth-grade standards by 2004.

One of the new developments in high school education in Ohio, begun in the 1990–91 school year, is aimed primarily at college-bound students. Called Postsecondary Enrollment Options, the acceleration mechanism permits high school students with the requisite grade ranks not only to substitute college courses for high school courses toward graduation, but also to earn college credit at the same time. To further reward students with high grades, upper tier students (top 20 percent) may take the college courses tuition-free, while students whose grades are in the next tier (top 40 percent) must pay for tuition, fees, and textbooks. The options at first were open only to high school juniors and seniors, but in 1998 the alternatives were extended to freshmen and sophomores. Another high school program geared to guide students into higher education is Tech Prep, which lets high school juniors design a curriculum that leads to an associate's degree at a college. Cooperation among colleges and universities, high schools, and industries smooths the transition from course work to applying that knowledge in the workplace.

GOAL #3—COMPETENCY AND TESTING FOR ALL

Ohio tests its students in grades four, six, nine, and twelve in five core subjects: writing, reading, citizenship, mathematics and science. For the most recent school year for which complete data are available, 1998, Ohio recorded these achievements:

1. Students in all the tested grades on average scored higher on the writing section of the proficiency tests than in 1996. Ninth

graders even surpassed the goal of a 90 percent passage rate when 94 percent passed in 1998.

2. In reading, the scores for students in all the tested grades on average improved over 1996. The 1998 ninth graders also exceeded the passage goal of 90 percent when 92 percent passed the reading test.

3. Citizenship and math scores remained the same for fourth graders, but improved at all other grade levels.

4. Science scores improved at every grade level.

5. Performance on the fourth-grade reading test is of particular importance because its passage will be a prerequisite to admission to fifth grade beginning Fall 1999 in a reform titled the Fourth Grade Guarantee. In 1998, 48 percent of the fourth graders passed the reading test, up from 46 percent in 1996 but still down from the highwater mark of 52 percent in 1997. The fourth graders are not put into a read-or-retain situation, however. Reading tests administered at the end of first, second, and third grade spot those who need remediation, including summer remediation and attempts to involve parents in the tutoring efforts. Students who have already repeated fourth grade may be promoted to fifth grade despite a failing score on the reading test if the principal and teacher agree to it. Yet the promotion decisions must now be governed by written policies.

6. Urban districts are still scoring below the state averages, but they are logging improved scores over the 1991 benchmarks.

7. Even though the largest number of Ohio students since 1989 took the American College Test (ACT) in 1998, the score average of 21.4 was above the national average of 21. Top score is 36.

8. On the Scholastic Aptitude Test (SAT), taken by a record 25 percent of Ohio high school students, scores were also above national averages and the highest average on Ohio record in math at 540. Top score is 800. It should be noted that longitudinal data for both the ACT and SAT reflect an inverse relationship between scores and numbers of students taking the tests. That is, when more students take a test, the scores are usually lower.

Ohio students countermanded that trend by logging higher scores even though more students took the tests.

9. The number of Ohio high school students who took Advanced Placement exams also increased in 1998, to more than 20,000 students taking 30,000 tests. A score of 3, 4, or 5 on a 5-point AP exam earns the student college credit, and Ohioans did that on more than 19,800 tests.

In one initiative similar to the School-to-Work coordination by the Bureau of Employment Services, the Department of Education administered the Career Passport program. Governor Voinovich put his imprimatur on the procedure for high schoolers that goes beyond preparing for the "productive employment" phrase of Goal #3. Steps in the process include preparing a resume and collecting pertinent data on the student's part, but the writing portion and the thinking it demands aim more at the "learn to use their minds well" standard of Goal #3. In an assignment called "validation of performance," the student must write three pieces of prose: (1) a career narrative, including the student's goals as well as career-related experiences, (2) a description of the student's skills, including competencies in specific areas, and (3) an essay demonstrating two of five employability skills, such as time management and interpersonal skills. The Career Passport program, which incorporates input from business people, educators, and students, was designed to go beyond prodding students to think about careers. The end product should be presentable enough to include as a portfolio item in a student's job search.

The proficiency tests administered in Ohio schools are not merely yardsticks to compare schools or to prove that schools are working harder and smarter. To use a testing term, the process is also diagnostic, revealing where efforts need to be redoubled. Statewide, all districts are required to provide summer remediation for any student who fails three of the five sections on the fourth- and sixth-grade proficiency tests. Three other examples exemplify statewide troubleshooting in 1997. One such remedy is the Comprehensive Intervention Strategy (CIS), which puts extra state money to work in 127 districts where student scores on proficiency tests are low. Independent performance audits (mentioned earlier in the Urban Schools Initiative) are available to the 127 CIS districts, urban and rural, that need help devising new strategies for improvement. One other tactic for boosting scores in 1997 evolved in two fourth-grade Urban Teacher Academies. Curriculum ideas and instructional strategies that may work better in imparting proficiency-test material were then shared by academy participants with other teachers.

GOAL #4—TEACHING HARDER AND SMARTER

"People still ask me why today's teachers aren't as good as they were thirty years ago. I tell them that today's teachers are better. The fact is, they face enormous challenges not confronted by their predecessors. And that is why we must do even more to help them," Governor Voinovich said in 1997. Perhaps the most dramatic change in teacher certification in Ohio during the Voinovich administration was the elimination of traditional certification. As Governor Voinovich said in the 1994 State of the State Address, "I still believe we need a common sense system that grants licenses only to those people who have demonstrated that they can teach, evaluates teacher performance regularly, intervenes when improvement is necessary, and ultimately removes those few who do not or cannot improve."

In the past, prospective teachers completed degrees in colleges of education, did a practice teaching stint under a certified teacher, then took a test on subject matter and instructional methods. Passing the test could mean lifetime certification in Ohio, in much the same way that lawyers pass the bar exam or physicians pass board certification. But even those professions are demanding continuing education of license holders. Starting in 1998, a new system of graduated licensure contingent on peer review debuted in Ohio to ensure that professional development does not end when teachers begin their profession.

The licensure process works this way. First, colleges of education in Ohio must meet standards of the National Council for the Accreditation of Teacher Education. Graduates of these colleges of education get a two-year provisional license. For those two years the newly minted teacher is assigned a mentor in the school where both teach. Before progressing to the next level of licensure, which is a five-year professional license, the teacher undergoes peer assessment using standards developed by the state. (The standards for the most widely used assessments are known by the acronym PRAXIS.) Holders of the professional license have ten years to complete either a master's degree in their area of specialization or thirty semester hours beyond the bachelor's degree. Holders of traditional certificates may renew their certificates only once before complying with the new rules. Key to license or certificate renewal is professional development in a planned fashion based on the needs of students, schools, and districts, as well as the teacher.

In fact, local Professional Development Committees whose function is to aid the alignment of teacher needs with school improvement goals will be required in every district effective with the 1998–99 school year. Because the job of serving the profession as mentor or assessor is time consuming and demanding, the Voinovich administration won legislative approval to compensate the seasoned teachers with a $1,500 annual stipend for mentors and $2,500 annual stipend for assessors.

Some of the appropriation pays for mentor/assessor training at Regional Professional Development Centers, twelve of which have been established since 1991 with Governor Voinovich's endorsement. The regional centers, which provide training in teaching methods, new technologies, and curriculum updates, feature a novel governance structure. Each center is overseen by a board comprised of teachers, administrators, higher education faculty, and business personnel. So far the centers have served as many as 20,000 teachers (approximately 20 percent of all Ohio teachers)—a number destined to increase as new licensure stipulations deploy throughout the profession.

The mentor/assessor process is also being applied to teachers who entered the profession under the old certification process. Several districts in the state are experimenting with Peer Review programs to help teachers improve their skills or—leave the profession. The Voinovich administration secured $1.8 million to supply the training for those districts wishing to try Peer Review. Governor Voinovich pointed out the necessity for continuing education for teachers in the 1997 State of the State Address. "We must provide our teachers with additional opportunities for professional development and growth. We've redefined education to mean lifelong learning—and it should certainly apply to those whose profession is to help others learn and succeed in life."

Though the term *certification* is outdated at the state level, at the national level certification is something of a badge of honor. Governor Voinovich thought well enough of the National Board of Professional Teaching Standards certification process that he recommended paying Ohio teachers just to try for it. Even better than the state's payment of the application fee (cost is about $1,000) is the outright reward of $2,500 to every teacher who gets national certification. A third incentive is the establishment of centers at twelve colleges of education for the purpose of coaching teachers through national certification rigors. Governor Voinovich went to Washington to recognize the first two Ohio teachers awarded national certification in 1995. By 1997 Ohio had 151 nationally certified teachers. The tally in late 1998 is 337, a total that puts Ohio second in the nation in the number of teachers earning national certification. Governor Voinovich had insisted on such eminence in the 1993 State of the State Address when he said, "We're going to make sure that Ohio's teachers are the best in the world."

> *"We're going to make sure that Ohio's teachers are the best in the world."*

GOAL #5—QUINTESSENTIAL CHALLENGES OF MATH AND SCIENCE

Will America realize its goal of attaining world leadership in math and science scores of students by the year 2000? No. Will Ohio? No, but scores are inching upward. Also significant in the effort to improve is Ohio's adoption of methods in math and science that work in nations earning the top scores. The Third International Mathematics and Science Study (TIMSS) reports the scores of participating nations and also gathers information about curriculum and instruction methods used in the top-scoring nations. What does work? More focus on fundamental principles in math and science, fewer topics taught in greater depth, and showing relationships among the fundamental concepts. Ohio embarked on conscious imitation of the TIMSS analysis in 1994 in the Model Competency-Based Education programs in math and science. Another teaching improvement vehicle is Project Discovery, cofunded by the National Science Foundation and the General Assembly beginning in 1992. Aimed at middle-level math and science teachers, the project trains teachers to use "inquiry-based instruction," which lets teams of students solve problems that have real-world applications. Underway is an effort to train up to 4,500 teachers in Project Discovery methods at the Regional Professional Development Centers. A third math-science initiative that began in 1998, Project SMART, takes a radical approach to instruction by pooling talent and ideas within an entire region of the state. Within twenty-one districts in Northeast Ohio, teams of teachers—along with industry and community representatives—devise strategies to democratize math and science for settings other than classrooms or offices viewed traditionally as the elite provinces of those studies.

GOAL #6—REACHING ADULTS BEYOND THE SCHOOLHOUSE

The efforts during the Voinovich administration to meet the goal of adults who can "compete in a global economy" are explained under the subhead of Workforce Development in the preceding chapter. Adult literacy, however, is another matter, one that has been an ongoing effort through the Adult Basic and Literacy Education (ABLE) programs under the aegis of the Department of Education. What was new during the Voinovich years, though, was an increase in enrollment in ABLE by Ohio Works First participants, who are required by law to get a high school degree or equivalency. Also, ten hours per week of the thirty-hour OWF work requirement may be satisfied with education that enhances employability. In the fall of 1998 a new statewide program called the Family Literacy Initiative joined the various literacy efforts run by private sector agencies. Sponsored by the Department of Education, the dual-generation initiative pairs adult learners with children so that families read together.

GOAL #7—ENVIRONMENTS CONDUCIVE TO LEARNING

To take on society outside the school is not the task at hand in meeting the national education goal on substance abuse and violence. The given is that substance abuse and violence among youths are widespread, as surveys and studies in every state thoroughly reveal. The plainly worded introductory phrase—"Every school will be free"—focuses on schools as havens from drugs, violence, firearms, and alcohol. To that end, Ohio's state agencies work on several fronts.

The Office of Criminal Justice Services (OCJS) has three programs focused specifically on Goal #7. Though the office's community-oriented policing has a broad scope statewide, one phase is devoted to training School Resource Officers (SROs). OCJS made $600,000 in grant money available to local law enforcement agencies to use for community policing projects in schools. A second effort by OCJS that affects school safety is its Violence Prevention Center, which was created in 1995 and is detailed in Chapter Five. Among the Center's activities is the production of information kits for schools. Titled "Promoting Peace in Your School: A Violence Prevention Action Kit," the packets have been sent to every school in Ohio. The kits include specific advice to teachers, students and parents on preventing violence, information brochures designed to be copied and distributed and how-to guides on school conflict management. Separate from the kits are the Center's annual anti-violence posters, which are sent to all middle and high schools in the state. Following the Governor's Task Force on Gun Violence, OCJS secured $5 million to provide security equipment for 174 schools, such as security lighting, cameras, electronic locking systems, fencing, and other hardware.

Programs in other agencies approach the substance abuse and violence issues from different angles. One approach is to promote rational responses when tensions arise. The Department of Education jointly sponsors training programs with the Ohio Commission on Dispute Resolution and Conflict Management to show teachers how to defuse potentially violent conflicts in school. Teachers can also take companion courses in the Ohio Violence Prevention Process sponsored by the state Department of Alcohol and Drug Addiction Services, an agency that also administers federal grant money in a pilot mentoring program begun in 1997 aimed at preventing use of illegal substances by youths. Other prevention and intervention services are available through the School Readiness Resource Centers sponsored by Governor Voinovich's Ohio Family and Children First initiative. Within the classroom itself is the option for teachers to try the Ohio Classroom Management System, an approach that teaches students why certain behaviors are unacceptable. Last, the two departments of Education and Alcohol and Drug Addiction Services administer grants supplied by the federal Safe and Drug-Free Schools and Communities Act to districts for designing prevention programs.

GOAL #8—PARENTS MOBILIZE IN PARTNERSHIPS

Parent-teacher associations are not new in education, but the nature of the relationship has progressed since Goal #8 (added to the national list in 1994) ensconced parents in decision making at school. Further emphasizing the importance of parental involvement is the fact that new teachers are evaluated in part by how well they communicate with parents. In Ohio, the Department of Education created a new Office of Family and School Partnerships in 1996 to coordinate existing programs and create new ones. Among the existing programs, some of which also fit in the early-childhood category, were (1) GRADS, the in-school program for pregnant and parenting teens described earlier, (2) TOPS, a statewide network of trainers who teach parents how to tutor their children, (3) Parents as Teachers, or PAT, a program that sends certified educators into homes to show parents of children from birth to age three how to encourage learning, (4) Even Start, a family literacy program similar to the Family Literacy Initiative except that Even Start focuses on early childhood education, and (5) Family Ties, a parent-education program for families with disabled children.

Meeting the goal, however, would require new ideas beyond strengthening parenting skills, ones that would involve parents in the decision making in schools. In 1996 a statewide Parent Involvement Summit helped shape the course of new venues for dialogue between parents and educators. The next year a more permanent structure was put in place with the statewide Parent Advisory Council, which will advise the Department of Education on future partnership efforts. Some ideas, though, are already being tested, such as home visits by teachers and principals, parent assistance in classrooms, in-school parent resource centers, and Home-School Compacts that put teachers, parents, and students in league to promise improvement. At the state level, one Department of Education response to parents' attempts to get involved was hiring an ombudsman, an objective third party who could advise parents how to channel concern about school into proper action. Broader in scope is the Ohio Parent Information and Resource Center (OhioPIRC), accessible to anyone by dialing 1-800-686-1738. The multifunctional School Readiness Resource Centers of Ohio Family and Children First, mentioned in earlier discussions about urban areas and school safety, also provide a host of services to pair up parents and children as partners in learning.

One partnership in parental involvement goes a generation farther. The Seniors Teaching and Reaching Students (STARS) program, administered by the Ohio Department of Aging, brings senior citizens into elementary schools as volunteer mentors and tutors. The program began in 1997 in nine communities, with twenty scheduled for the 1998–99 school year.

The job of increasing parental involvement is not over. At this writing, the Department of Education is working to improve on four fronts: (1) defining parental involvement more clearly, (2) getting more parents of high school age students involved, (3) helping Ohio Works First parents stay involved with their children's education, and (4) refining measures of quantity and quality of parental involvement.

OPERATIONS IMPROVEMENT
ADMITTED TO COLLEGE

Ohio institutions of higher learning underwent the same examination during the early Voinovich years that every other state body did, only a different group of people did the review. Instead of asking the cadre of unpaid volunteers on the Operations Improvement Task Force to take on collegial models of management, too, Governor Voinovich asked the Ohio Board of Regents to draft people familiar with the complexities of college and university operations to recommend ways to work harder and smarter. The OIT-style review group for colleges was called the Managing for the Future Task Force. Nineteen leaders from higher education, communities, government, and business made up the A team, while B teams were constituted to conduct a companion review at each individual campus.

Here's the situation they reviewed: sixty-two institutions of higher education, categorized into thirteen four-year universities, twenty-four branch campuses, fifteen community colleges, eight technical colleges, and two medical schools unaffiliated with universities. Estimated total enrollment in the later 1990s is about one-third of a million full-time equivalents (FTE). While higher education depends on its customers to pay up front, tuition nationally provides an average of about 30 percent of an institution's budget. (Ohio ranked thirty-ninth in the nation in state spending for higher education in 1994 and ninth highest in tuition.) Endowments and gifts, invested in instruments of varying predictability, also vary widely across and within institutions. Thus the state provides the bulk of the money for publicly supported colleges and universities. For Ohio's sixty-two postsecondary schools, that bulk is the third largest item in the state budget. In FY 1999 the total General Revenue Fund budget for higher education was $2.3 billion. In fact, between 1991 and 1999, higher education's budget rose 34.8 percent, according to data from the Office of Budget and Management, while inflation rose 25.9 percent in the same time.

In the same way that QStP spun off the OIT review process as a response to the call for quality, the report titled *Securing the Future* was crafted by the Ohio Board of Regents in response to the Managing for the Future report. *Securing the Future* grappled with three challenges facing higher education: (1) balancing quality and affordability in higher education, (2) ensuring access to higher education for all Ohioans, and (3) upgrading the research mission of colleges and universities. The report also suggested specific areas for closer scrutiny: a statewide review of doctoral programs, a study of faculty workload policies, and a call for tying funding at two-year campuses to service expectations.

"My hat is off to Ohio's colleges and universities, which have accepted the challenge to cut costs and refocus their missions."

By 1994, colleges and universities were turning in results. In the State of the State Address that year, Governor Voinovich acknowledged their efforts: "My hat is off to Ohio's colleges and universities, which have accepted the challenge to cut costs and refocus their missions as laid out in the Board of Regents' *Securing the Future* report and recommendations from their individual Operations Improvement Task Forces. Already, new efficiency measures are saving millions of dollars on campuses across the state—duplicate courses and subject majors are being consolidated or cut altogether—and, thanks to your efforts, undergraduate faculty members are spending more time where our students need them most—in the classroom."

On the affordability front, Governor Voinovich sought and got legislative limits on tuition, in his first and subsequent budgets. The caps resulted in average tuition increases of only 4.3 percent in the five years between 1993 and 1998, compared to the average increase of 6.9 percent between 1983 and 1990. That 38 percent reduction in increases did its job in enhancing access to Ohio's colleges and universities.

Accessibility to higher education was boosted in the form of financial aid, both need-based and merit-based to keep outstanding students from leaving the state. The increase in aid across the last eight years has been 105 percent. The governor and legislature concurred on increases in the following types of student assistance:

1. Ohio Instructional Grants, awarded to students whose income and family size create financial need, increased 85.8 percent in the eight years Governor Voinovich was in office. More than 90,000 students have received grants from the pool that grew from $51.8 million in FY 1991 to $96.3 million in FY 1999.

2. Part-time Ohio Instructional Grants, as the name implies, are designed for non-traditional students. Begun in 1993, the program used almost $11.9 million in FY 1999 to serve about 35,000 students.

3. War Orphans Scholarship Program, also open to children of veterans, grew from $2 million in FY 1991 to $3.8 million in FY 1999 to serve 900 students.

4. Academic Scholarships are $2,000-per-year awards to persuade Ohioans to stay in the state for college. This particular scholarship pool represents the largest growth among the state's finan-

cial aid vehicles—222 percent. It grew from $3.6 million in FY 1991 to $8 million in FY 1999.

5. Student Choice Grants enable Ohio's array of private colleges and universities to keep Ohioans in-state. The grant amount per student per year has increased from $578 to $924 from FY 1991 to 1999. (The tuition for a full load for one year at a four-year public university in Ohio is about $3,000 on average. Private schools cost more.)

Incentives were offered to institutions of higher learning for meeting performance standards. Under the Performance Challenge program, for example, two-year colleges already have measures and goals to meet. Some of these are to enroll students in specific career preparation programs; to build partnerships with business, industry, and the community; to provide continuing education; to help students prepare to transfer to four-year colleges; to improve student access to higher education; and to establish relationships with high schools for better articulation of student curriculum. (Articulation means ensuring that courses in a sequence or curriculum fit together coherently.)

Six other functions of colleges and universities deemed in need of improvement were later subject to the Performance Challenge model, with supplements to the instructional subsidy based on performance measures.

1. The Research Challenge uses state seed money (as matching funds or loans) to attract research grants from other sources, particularly for research with economic development potential.

2. The Access Challenge ties supplemental funds to measured improvements in access to two-year community colleges and urban center campuses.

3. The Jobs Challenge supplements are based on a college's expenditures on workforce training and development.

4. The Technology Challenge uses state money to encourage the use of technology to improve teaching and productivity.

5. The Success Challenge rewards those colleges that seek to increase the success rates of students considered at-risk in the higher education setting.

6. The Efficiency Challenge rewards measurable improvements in getting more for the dollar to colleges that demonstrate greater efficiency.

One new effort in Ohio's higher education improvement process is a collaboration with high schools to help students enter college better prepared. The Secondary and Higher Education Remediation Advisory Commission (SHERAC) announced its plan in 1997 to boost college readiness by working toward consensus between secondary and higher education on the very definition of "college level" standards in reading, writing, and mathematics.

Just as education for kindergarten through twelfth grade gets priority in state spending over colleges and universities, undergraduate education now takes precedence over graduate school spending. What was intended as a disincentive to increases in post-baccalaureate admissions were enrollment caps applied in FY 1996. The amount of state support for doctoral programs and law schools was capped at FY 1995 enrollment levels. It was more than a matter of relative merit of levels of education. The funding formula for higher education in Ohio pays more per graduate student than for undergraduates. A clear trend of enrollment increases had emerged. In the fiscal years 1991 to 1995, graduate-level enrollment increased 45 percent while overall growth was just 6.6 percent. The dollar increase was understandably even higher because of the larger amounts tied to graduate enrollment—up 55 percent for the same period while overall instructional support was up 4.5 percent. The Board of Regents also reviewed the state's 117 doctoral programs in eleven disciplines. The ax fell on ten doctoral programs. Sixteen others were narrowed. The savings total to the state was estimated by the Office of Budget and Management at $14 million. One other aspect of new law required the Board of Regents to develop workload standards for full- and part-time teaching faculty. The 1993 law also required a 10 percent increase in undergraduate teaching by fall 1994. (A ruling by the Ohio Supreme Court in September 1998 overturned the faculty workload law at the two colleges in Ohio with teacher unions, Central State University and Shawnee State University.)

Governor Voinovich had asked for and gotten results. In the 1997 State of the State Address he reported, "Our two-year colleges are doing better than ever before at meeting the education and training needs of their local communities and represent the most unsung economic development tool we have. And I meet more and more Ohioans who tell me that the quality education offered by our state colleges and universities is the best education value in America. And in a recent national survey, ten of our thirteen public universities were ranked among the best in the nation."

EDUCATION FOR PREVENTION—DEGREES OF ALCOHOL AND DRUG USE

Much of the work of the Department of Alcohol and Drug Addiction Services (ODADAS) is educational in purpose but is conducted outside schools. From preschoolers to collegians to workers on the job, ODADAS programs aim to teach prevention as the prescription to head off abuse and possible addiction to alcohol and drugs. The ODADAS education effort that gets the most attention in the media is the international Parents Resource Institute for Drug Education (PRIDE) conferences in Cincinnati. More than 17,000 educators, parents, youth, business, and government officials met in 1993 and 1996 to update their knowledge about drug prevention. In late 1998 ODADAS was gearing up for the 1999 international PRIDE conference scheduled for Cincinnati in April.

Another program administered by ODADAS is unique in the nation. The Urban Minority Alcoholism and Drug Abuse Outreach Programs (UMADs) served more than 120,000 African- and Hispanic-

American youth in FY 1996 by pairing youth with minority leaders in their respective communities. Early childhood prevention education aimed at preschoolers is conducted by ODADAS for Head Start administrators. Since 1995, the department has trained about 120 Head Start staffers in four workshops per year.

For older students there is the Ohio model for binge drinking prevention on college campuses, also administered by ODADAS in conjunction with the Department of Public Safety. In 1997, the department provided grant money for nineteen colleges with incidences of binge drinking to participate in training seminars through Ohio Parents for Drug Free Youth. Campus-based teams of students, community representatives and substance abuse coordinators learned about building coalitions, social marketing, and policy formulation in order to educate others about the scourge of drinking-to-get-drunk that is sweeping college campuses nationwide.

Media campaigns to spread the anti-drug message were developed by ODADAS with the Partnership for a Drug Free America beginning in 1993. Public service announcements aired in the five largest markets in Ohio often enough to rank in the nation's top fifteen for air time donated to the campaign. By 1996 the value of the PSAs— had they been purchased at regular advertising rates—was figured at more than $1 billion by ODADAS. Another partnership in agency education was forged in 1991 by ODADAS and the Department of Education to distribute free information on the dangers of drugs and alcohol. The first Ohio Prevention and Education Resource Center opened in Cincinnati in 1991, but spun off satellite offices in Columbus, Cleveland, and Toledo. The Department of Public Safety has joined the other two agencies as the third OPERC partner.

LIFELONG LEARNING IN OTHER STATE AGENCIES

Governor Voinovich sought to increase the education level of Ohioans within the executive agencies of the state as well as in schools. One program called Personal Enrichment through Education (PETE) provides instruction in reading, writing, and mathematics for state employees who are prepping for the Graduate Equivalency Diploma (GED) or who simply want to improve their basic skills. PETE is administered by the Department of Administrative Services.

"Finer with Age" is a monthly television program with an education function for senior citizens. Available via community and public access stations, the show provides information on issues and programs salient to seniors. Begun in 1993 in the Department of Aging, the forty episodes of "Finer with Age" have won four awards in the Columbus area. Information in depth for older Ohioans is available in *Ohio's Heritage,* a quarterly magazine distributed to more than 51,000 households. The information and entertainment magazine has won two major awards: from the International Association of Business Communicators (in 1995 and 1996) and from the National Mature Media Awards (in 1995).

Information about the stability and economic contributions of Ohio's family farms is available through the Outstanding Century Farms Awards Program. Partnered by the Department of Agriculture, the *Ohio Country Journal,* and the Ohio Historical Society, the program began in 1993 as an educational venture about farming.

Teaching future generations about the role of military veterans is the purpose of the Ohio Veterans Hall of Fame, established by Governor Voinovich in 1992 after endorsement by a blue-ribbon panel of veterans the governor had asked to review the plans. Enshrined at the first induction were the six Ohio military veterans who served as President of the United States (Can you name them?) and the 317 Ohio Congressional Medal of Honor recipients. The Veterans Hall of Fame moved in 1996 to its permanent location in Sandusky at the Ohio Veterans Home. (Answer: William Henry Harrison, Ulysses S. Grant, Rutherford B. Hayes, James A. Garfield, Benjamin Harrison, William McKinley.)

School teachers aren't the only state employees whose licensure requirements include continuing education. During Governor Voinovich's tenure, insurance agents licensed in Ohio were required by law to complete a minimum number of classroom hours to remain current on insurance issues and new insurance products.

Most people think of the role of the Ohio Lottery in education as purely financial. While 15.5 percent of the state funding for public schools does come from the Lottery, in addition, the agency sponsors workshops and communications through its Problem Gambling Awareness Department in conjunction with the Ohio Council on Problem Gambling.

The Department of Rehabilitation and Correction (DRC) operates its own brand of schools within Ohio penal institutions. In fact, one of the newer prisons is devoted entirely to education—the Montgomery Education and Pre-Release Center in Dayton. Though the application of distance learning via television and computer has improved options for instruction, more teachers were needed. Between 1991 and 1998 the number of teaching staff increased from 302 to 532. The more literate inmates helped by joining the teachers as tutors for fellow-inmates. In thirty-nine multidisciplinary literacy units, 2,400 "students" were assisted by 1,200 "teachers"—all of them inmates. DRC also increased the number of inmate apprenticeships from 136 to 674 between 1991 and 1998. In another innovation, DRC established a mentoring model in partnership with the Prince Hall Masonic Lodge.

The Bureau of Workers' Compensation seminars and workshops cover a range of workplace issues beyond job training. For example, the Division of Safety and Hygiene offers courses in such diverse topics as "Confined Space Assessment and Work," "Basic Industrial Noise and Hearing Conservation," "Hazardous Waste Awareness," and "Scaffolding Safety" in its continuing education efforts at regional BWC centers.

The governor recapped his efforts for education in the 1998 State of the State Address. "Together, we have traveled an incredible distance since 1991. Across the education waterfront—from performance to accountability, technology, professional development and school funding—we have acted responsibly and rewritten the history books."

CHAPTER 5

Quality of Life

"Most Ohioans have had enough welfare, enough poverty, enough drugs, enough crime. Most would love to see that debilitating cycle broken, and the people trapped within it freed, once and for all. So would I. The only way to do it is to pick one generation of children, draw a line in the sand, and say to all: 'This is where it stops.'"

HONORING OHIO'S FIRST LADY

GEORGE VOINOVICH PRAISED his wife in the February 1998 State of the State Address: "Janet Voinovich is a person who loves and cares deeply for her fellow citizens. I've always thought of Janet as God's greatest blessing on me. The truth is, she's also been a blessing on Ohio. With grace and vigor, she works tirelessly for our children and families, and I think it's appropriate to honor her service." Those words in a public speech were not her sole honor. First Lady Janet Voinovich stood in the limelight at Ohio University in mid-September 1998 to receive the highest honor bestowed by the College of Osteopathic Medicine in Athens—the Phillips Medal of Public Service. The

125

list of causes she has advocated—the Ronald McDonald House, Adopt-a-School, *Help Me Grow,* the campaign to detect breast cancer, intergenerational programs in schools, to name the most significant—led to the description of Mrs. Voinovich as "the first mother of Ohio" at the Ohio University awards ceremony. While the governor increased expenditures for families and children in every budget he presented, the voice of Mrs. Voinovich in the official chorus confirmed Ohio's proactive commitment to help those who need help the most.

OHIO'S FIRST PRIORITY—FAMILIES AND CHILDREN

"Most Ohioans have had enough welfare, enough poverty, enough drugs, enough crime. Most would love to see that debilitating cycle broken, and the people trapped within it freed, once and for all. So would I. The only way to do it is to pick one generation of children, draw a line in the sand, and say to all: 'This is where it stops.'" In one of his most widely quoted expressions, Governor Voinovich prefaced a plan in his second year as governor that broke the mold in government's traditional ways of delivering services to families and children. The governor said in his 1992 State of the State Address about Ohio Family and Children First, "This [initiative] will be driven by locally based providers, not bureaucrats in Columbus. And it will develop a plan to meet the health, education, and social service needs of disadvantaged children and families, and develop an action plan to meet those needs by eliminating barriers, coordinating programs, and targeting dollars." Ohio Family and Children First (OFCF), then, set in stone the line the governor had drawn in the sand one year earlier to change conditions for the next generation of children.

The overall purpose of OFCF is to achieve Goal #1 in the list of national education goals—All children in American will start school ready to learn. In Ohio, achieving the goal has been operationalized by focusing on three variables that affect a child's ability to learn: (1) putting a preschooler in situations where learning is lauded, (2) assuring the physical health of the child, and (3) improving the child's emotional environment by aiding family stability. The ambitious plans of OFCF to give the minds, bodies, and hearts of children the best possible foundation is clearly beyond the purview of departments of education and schools. Ohio Family and Children First bridged the gaps.

Chapter 4 discussed the actions in Ohio to provide access to preschools, Head Start programs, and readiness centers that give children and their parents opportunities to acclimate to a school setting (such as a teacher reading to children) as well as to launch academic pursuits (such as discussing the reading with children). The two other prongs of the OFCF initiative—health and family—required new thinking, new money, and new efforts. The new thinking took a form that should be familiar to a reader of Voinovichiana at this point—partnerships, new alignments between public and private organizations. In addition, OFCF sought better coordination between old partners, state and local governments, so that their circles of influence intersect for maximum flexibility and unison. The new money was approved by the legislature, but new ways to shepherd it were built into OFCF strategy as objectives and measures of improvement. New efforts were focused on prevention and intervention as preferable to remediation ten or twenty years hence in the life of a child. The ultimate goal in every case is to put every child squarely over the line in the sand toward eventual self-sufficiency.

Here's how OFCF is structured. Approved by the General Assembly in 1993, an OFCF Cabinet Council was established to provide guidance. Chaired by Governor Voinovich, the Cabinet Council consists of the Superintendent of Public Instruction and the directors of pertinent state agencies: Alcohol and Drug Addiction Services, Budget and Management, Health, Human Services, Mental Health, Mental Retardation and Developmental Disabilities, and Youth Services. Though not mandated and therefore strictly voluntary, local Family and Children First councils have been created in all eighty-eight Ohio counties. Members of the local councils are county-level counterparts of the state-level agencies, plus members from the ranks of Head Start grantees, representatives of not-for-profit organizations, judges, county commissioners, and others whose interest leads them to volunteer. At least three people on the council must be family members whose sole reason for OFCF involvement is the strengthening of families. The point of the structure, of course, is to increase, or in some cases initiate, cooperation among organizations with similar functions and perhaps the same clients. The county councils receive minimal funding from the state ($20,000 in FY 1999) for staff support, parent stipends, training, and retreats. The state, however, provides personnel in the form of loaned executives from the eight state agencies of the Cabinet Council, who provide technical assistance specific to the agencies' functions and who form a network among the eight agencies back in Columbus.

In one aspect of OFCF that could be described as rule-testing, the Cabinet Council reviews requests by local councils to waive specific state rules in order to try innovations in service delivery. Eighteen such waivers had been approved by 1998. Evaluation measures on the innovations will be scrutinized to determine if the rules that were temporarily waived might be eliminated altogether. Another experimental device, the State Intersystem Fund, is designed to reduce the compound costs incurred when clients use the services of several agencies. Formerly called Cluster, the new accounting allots more money to local councils for solutions that keep children and families out of expensive institutions.

Other state-level personnel provided to the OFCF effort are ten regional coordinators who provide leadership on broader issues of governance, evaluation, program design and management, and client relations in the five OFCF regions of the state. The loaned executives and the regional coordinators comprise the OFCF Action Team.

PROACTIVE PARTNERSHIPS
FOR HELPING CHILDREN GROW

To educate would-be clients about health issues and services available, OFCF launched *Help Me Grow*, which is both an information campaign and the title of a booklet chockfull of information about prenatal and well-baby care, child development, child safety, foster care and adoption, preventing child abuse and neglect, and how to find resources close at hand to assist with all those issues. And according to the experts in health-care provider associations and other pertinent organizations who've endorsed the campaign, the information is accurate and clear. For example, an August 1998 booklet available in Kroger stores lists times, locations, and dates for free vaccinations, plus a simply written message explaining that a second measles, mumps, and rubella immunization (MMR) is required by state law for seventh graders. *Help Me Grow* is distributed free in many settings (e.g., physicians' offices, preschools, and Early Childhood Centers) and is cosponsored with the state by such corporations as Ronald McDonald House Charities of Central Ohio, McDonald's Corporation, Pfizer Incorporated, the Kroger Company, Marshall Field's, LensCrafters, and Nationwide Health Plans. The *Help Me Grow* campaign has also benefited from a total of $3 million in cash and in-kind contributions since 1995 from national philanthropic foundations as well as from the federal government. Official spokesperson for the statewide *Help Me Grow* campaign is First Lady Janet Voinovich.

Help Me Grow also disseminates information via its 1-800 helpline, which had logged 163,000 calls by 1998. Of those callers, 76,000 were linked to services such as low-cost health care and nutrition assistance. Though the initial focus of the helpline was prenatal and well-baby care, its scope has since broadened to include foster care, adoption, and other services. *Help Me Grow* also expanded to a third medium with the videotape titled *I Am Your Child*, which is given to the parents of all newborns in participating hospitals through a partnership with the Ohio Hospital Association. Sixty percent of Ohio hospitals were participating in the video giveaway by late 1998.

ACCOUNTING FOR ACHIEVEMENTS IN OFCF ACTIONS

The state has not relied solely on corporate and charitable benefactors to support Ohio Family and Children First programs. State spending on programs for children and families has increased 47 percent since 1991. (The upward line stands out in the prevailing pattern of downward lines under Governor Voinovich, who held state spending growth to its lowest level in thirty years.) The money is spent on the following services, for which OFCF has assigned itself measurable goals: prenatal care for moms eligible for Medicaid, alcohol and drug addiction treatment for newborns whose mothers used drugs, immunizations, services for children with disabilities ages birth to three, early childhood education, special education, reduction of placement of children in foster homes, promotion of adoptions, and reduction in the number of teen pregnancies. Data from OFCF in 1998 reveal the following measured results on each of the above expenditures:

1. Low-income women who initiated visits to Maternal and Child Health Clinics in their first trimester of pregnancy increased to 66 percent from 44.5 percent five years earlier. In the same time frame, the number of pregnant women using Medicaid's Healthy Start program tripled.

2. The number of drug-free babies born to women receiving treatment for alcohol or drug addiction has increased to 703 in FY 1998 from 156 in FY 1993. Since the average cost of treating an infant born to an alcohol- or drug-abusive mother is $46,000 in the first year of the infant's life, about $120 million has been saved through the intervention services provided to the nearly 2,611 drug-free babies born since the program began.

3. The number of fully immunized two-year-olds has reached the 77 percent level, up from 51 percent in 1991, while state spending on immunizations increased 279 percent—from $1.9 million in FY 1991 to $7.2 million in FY 1999. Additional funding from the Centers for Disease Control has enabled Ohio to provide immunizations for 128,000 children per year. Of significance is the fact that in 1997 there was not a single case of measles reported in the state of Ohio, a first. Starting in May 1997, OFCF saw to it that a registry of immunization was com-

piled in a database, complete with reminders to parents. Called IMPACT, the immunization tracking system saved the state money, too, thanks to a $390,000 grant from the Aetna Foundation.

4. Children with disabilities ages birth through three are evaluated only if their families volunteer, as explained earlier about the Early Start initiative. Of the families who consented to evaluation, 60 percent were served in 1996, up from 39.4 percent in 1992. TANF funds were used to expand the number of counties with Early Start visits. Plus, the program has put in place a mechanism to head off child abuse or neglect in situations long associated with that possibility. In addition, a "welcome home visit" has been funded for every teenage or first-time mother in Ohio.

5. Early childhood education was discussed earlier, but summary numbers bear repeating. The number of children in Head Start, Public Preschool and Preschool Special Education now surpasses 66,000, more than a ten-fold increase in five years, which makes Ohio the nation's leader in percent of eligible children served.

6. Preschool children with disabilities have the option of services individualized for them. In special education parlance, these Individual Education Plans are called IEPs. In 1990, only 18 percent of eligible children were served via IEPs. The percentage rose to 52 by 1996.

7. The number of children placed outside their homes (in foster care or institutions) has been reduced, due in part to the Family Stability Incentive Fund, a state and local partnership that offers incentive rewards for reducing the number of children placed outside the home. In the seventeen original OFCF counties, about 8,700 fewer children were diverted from out-of-home placement by summer 1998. The sixteen other OFCF counties who participate in the fund are on track toward meeting the goal of diverting 25 percent fewer children from out-of-home placements. Approximately 85 percent of Ohio children under the age

of eighteen reside in the thirty-three counties that participate in the Family Stability Incentive.

8. Adoptions in Ohio have increased 35 percent since 1990. In 1997, 1,465 children got new homes and families, up from 920 in 1990.

9. Reducing the number of teen pregnancies, the newest of the measures of family stability, has not yet been operationalized in reliable terms and was not undertaken until the 1996 Wellness Block Grants, provided by the state as an incentive to local OFCF councils, provided the necessary funding. The second function of the Wellness Block Grants will be to explore new ways to prevent child abuse and neglect.

As early as 1994 Governor Voinovich expressed pride in the OFCF progress in only one year. "I'm excited about our nine Family and Children First pilot projects in thirteen counties, which are helping us find local, homegrown solutions to cut government red tape, coordinate service delivery and assure that the dollars we spend on families are being spent wisely," he said in the State of the State Address that year. "Marion Wright Edelman of the Children's Defense Fund was kind enough to say, 'If every state had a governor that provided this level of leadership on children, we would be ready for the future.' It's nice that someone of her stature would notice—but, again, what's been accomplished so far in Ohio, we've done together."

To assure that infants are healthier . . .
In addition to the information campaign of *Help Me Grow* and the programs put in place to achieve the nine goals, several other efforts to boost health access for children are ongoing, many of them partnerships. On the welcome sign at the city limits of nearly every sizable town in America are the logos of the long-established organizations of Kiwanis and Rotary. For the first time in the history of these international service clubs, a partnership has been formed—in Ohio—to help OFCF promote childhood immunizations. In addition to enlisting club members who work in medical fields to spread

the word, the Kiwanis and Rotary members provide staffing at health fairs, county fairs, and other outreach opportunities.

The Medicaid expansion mentioned earlier affected thousands of Ohio children. As of January 1998, all children under the age of nineteen in families with income below 150 percent of the federal poverty level are eligible for Medicaid coverage. That adds more than a quarter of a million children (275,000, or about the population of the Akron metropolitan area) to those covered earlier by Medicaid expansion. Services available include Healthy Start; Early and Periodic Screening, Diagnosis, and Treatment (EPSDT); and the Medicaid in the Schools program. According to figures from the Office of Budget and Management, state and federal funding for Medicaid for children in FY 1999 will be $1.2 billion. Though it would be difficult to attempt an actuarial style assessment of how much money the $1.2 billion saves in future medical bills, it should be emphasized that such preventive medical care for children does head off costlier procedures later—and surely a lot of pain and suffering, too. In a related improvement, Ohio has streamlined its waiver process to allow children with severe conditions to remain at home rather than in a nursing home or hospital. About 1,200 children under the age of eighteen were affected by this 1998 change.

Gifts of Sight is an OFCF partnership that gives corrective eyewear to needy children. Prevent Blindness Ohio provides free eye exams while LensCrafters supplies vouchers for eyeglasses. When Lens-Crafters opened its 700th store, it celebrated by providing 700 eyewear vouchers that are distributed through Early Start, Family Resource Centers and School Readiness Resource Centers. The estimated value of a voucher is $125.

To improve services to strengthen families . . .
AdoptOhio, an experimental approach to increasing the number of children adopted, uses a strategy of payments at each step of the adoption process. Financial incentives are awarded to agencies that recruit and train adoptive families, make initial placements, finalize

adoption, and provide post-adoption services. Though all public children services agencies are required to participate, forty-three private agencies have also agreed to work harder to find families for more children. AdoptOhio provides prospective parents with a booklet, updated quarterly, of photos and information about children seeking to be adopted, plus a web site for faster updates. Since the incentives began in July 1997, 283 of the 1,400 adoptions that year in the state were directly attributable to AdoptOhio, according to OFCF documents.

Collecting child support from an absent parent is another of state government's attempts to strengthen single-parent families. In his first year in office, Governor Voinovich announced in-house searches for child-support deadbeats among state employees. The zero tolerance expanded to private businesses that sought to do business with the state. Then a deadbeat list was matched with income tax forms. The governor even put up "Most Wanted" posters to stigmatize parents who owed the most in back payments. While improving family strength on all fronts was one widely publicized motive, another reason the Voinovich administration pushed for child support payments was to bring Ohio into compliance with federal audit criteria. By 1997 collections had increased 70 percent over 1991, from $844 million to $1.43 billion. In the same time, the number of paternities established increased 74 percent. As mentioned in Chapter 2, Ohio won the Outstanding Program Achievement Award from the National Child Support Enforcement Association in 1996 for the state's various collection efforts.

Giving parents a respite from the strain of caring for disabled or traumatized children is the purpose of Project HELP. The goal is to provide breaks from the highly demanding jobs of caring for children with mental and physical disabilities, or children who have been abused or neglected. OFCF, along with the departments of Mental Health, Mental Retardation and Developmental Disabilities, Human Services, and Education, guides efforts in eight locations to create more community recess time for parents of these children. Begun in

1995, Project HELP has provided $820,000 for pilot projects in the counties of Athens, Cuyahoga, Lake, Licking, Putnam, Richland, Shelby, and Washington.

Locating children at risk, offering assistance, and gaining acceptance from families are the overall challenges of OFCF's Family Resource Centers. Operating out of schools, offices, or even mobile units, the Family Resources Centers are the front line against child abuse and neglect. Among the intervention services offered through the centers are home visitation, Head Start information, other preschool options, child development education for parents, intergenerational activities, mentoring, programs to promote health and avoid substance abuse, and workshops on job searches and skills training. Acceptance has been gained by bringing the beneficiaries of the programs and the community delivery-system workers into the decision making on the design, operation, and governance of the Family Resource Centers.

Delivering services to those who need them sometimes demands solutions as obvious as providing transportation. After all, forty counties in Ohio have no public transportation, and many of the clients of the state's social services have no vehicles of their own to get to a Family Resource Center, for example. The Department of Transportation therefore provides grants to counties so that service providers can coordinate efforts to move people to services or services to people. Called the Ohio Coordination Program, it began in 1997 as an offshoot of the move toward self-sufficiency required by welfare reform legislation in Ohio.

Assistance toward self-sufficiency for the disabled does not end at the preschool level in Ohio. Project LIFE (Linkages for Individual and Family Empowerment) takes up where public schools leave off for these older Ohio youths. A partnership among OFCF, the Department of Education, and the School-to-Work process, Project LIFE uses a teamwork approach to assist families of disabled students to find work or activities for these young people. In a related effort, the Putting People First self-determination project gives disabled individuals more say in deciding the direction of their paths toward self-sufficiency. In a new and decidedly experimental approach to giving the developmentally disabled increased control of their own lives, Putting People First brings the disabled into the decision making on how to shape their futures in career choices and living arrangements. Funded in part by the Robert Wood Johnson Foundation, Putting People First is administered by the Ohio Developmental Disabilities Planning Council.

Parent Leadership Training is just that—a civics curriculum to teach parents how to get and stay involved in government and public life to benefit both their families and communities. Parents attend a twenty-one-week program that includes all the help they need to overcome such attendance obstacles as child care, meals, and transportation. Each class then mentors the next class, a procedure that reinforces lessons for parents and builds parent networks for communities. By 1998 more than five hundred parents had participated in the Parent Leadership Training Institute in twenty Ohio counties, making it the largest effort of its kind in the nation.

A couple of ideas endorsed by OFCF benefit all families and not just those who need special services. Ohio extended maternity and paternity leave both for births and for adoptions to all state employees. Governor Voinovich proposed that the paid leave extend to adoptive parents to encourage adoptions and to fathers to encourage them to bond with their newborns. Since the six-week leave began in 1994, nearly 14,500 parents have used it. A later enhancement was the allowance of $2,000 paid to adoptive parents in lieu of leave to help defray adoption expenses. Another effort motivated by the desire to strengthen families is OFCF's negotiation with the Ohio State Fair to set aside two days as Family Days at the 1998 fair.

"So many of our families are vulnerable, and I am going to do everything in my power to protect them."

Ohio Family and Children First put into practice much of what Governor Voinovich had always preached. As he put it in the 1996 State of the State Address, "I've often said that if I had a magic wand to solve Ohio's problems, I would reconstitute the family. So many of our families are vulnerable, and I am going to do everything in my power to protect them." By the 1998 State of the State Address, he reported that two respected foundations (the Kaufman Foundation and the Pew Charitable Trust) were praising Ohio for doing more than any other state to fund early childhood services and to reform its social services and education systems.

WORKING HARDER AND WISER
FOR OHIO'S OLDER CITIZENS

The sole function of the Department of Aging in Ohio is "to improve the quality of life for older Ohioans." Under Governor Voinovich the department developed several innovations that improved quality of life patterns while saving money. The centerpiece is a trio of programs called collectively Community Care Choices Initiative (CCC), which is the long-term care component of Governor Voinovich's Medicaid reform strategy. Before the CCC reforms, nursing home costs consumed about half of the annual Medicaid bill for the state. To sum up, CCC aims to keep older citizens in their homes, to assist low-income elderly with care, and to educate seniors about their long-term care options.

In the 1993 State of the State Address Governor Voinovich announced: "I have great news for older Ohioans—our Washington office has just informed us that we've succeeded in our efforts to expand the PASSPORT program. This will enable us to triple our services by 1998. Most older Ohioans would rather stay in their homes and apartments, sur-

"Most older Ohioans would rather stay in their homes and apartments, surrounded by the loving care of their family and friends, and assisted by local services, which are so much more affordable than nursing homes—and it's our responsibility to help make that happen."

rounded by the loving care of their family and friends, and assisted by local services, which are so much more affordable than nursing homes—and it's our responsibility to help make that happen." From the comfort of their own homes, older Ohioans eligible for Medicaid can now receive a variety of community-based services through PASSPORT—meal delivery, personal care, physical therapy, health equipment, and transportation, to name some. The combination of services chosen is covered under Medicaid so long as the total does not exceed 60 percent of the costs of living in a nursing home for six months. (Average annual cost for living in a nursing home in the mid-1990s was $36,000.) PASSPORT is one of the most significant success stories in Ohio government during the Voinovich years. In 1991 PASSPORT served 2,700 eligible senior citizens statewide. By 1999 the total should reach 24,000—an 850 percent increase in eight years. That's almost 20,000 people spending 40 percent less on services, thanks to the in-home delivery. Saving money is of course good government, but improving quality of life should also be acknowledged, though it's hard to put a price tag on the peace of mind that is surely a by-product of PASSPORT.

For low-income older Ohioans with disabilities or frailties, the state offers the Residential State Supplement (RSS), which enables them to live in a more residential setting. These citizens need some assistance, but don't require the full-range, around-the-clock care available at nursing homes. The supplement boosts their incomes enough to live in an assisted-living facility. Since 1993, RSS enrollments have tripled from 900 to nearly 2,750.

The newest of the CCC trio is Care Choice Ohio, an information program to help aging people make informed decisions about their long-term care. The goal is to encourage older people to plan for their future needs with their families before the need is imminent. Available to any Ohioan regardless of income, Care Choice sends a professional in financial and care options for in-home consultations with those who request the service, which is free. Since Care Choice began in May 1996, more than 3,000 consultations have been completed. Of those served, 91 percent reported that they "learned something they had not known before," according to a Department of Aging survey.

Ohio's senior citizens gained other benefits during the Voinovich administration besides the Community Care Choices. One related initiative is the Senior Community Services Block Grant introduced in 1991 to provide enough services to help older people avoid certain Medicaid expenses. By combining six line items from previous budgets, the Voinovich administration created a block of money that local Area Agencies on Aging (AAAs) can distribute where needed. AAAs are consortia of nonprofit organizations that function in twelve multi-county Planning Service Areas throughout Ohio. The $13 million annual block grants purchase such services as transportation, home delivery of meals, adult day care, housekeeping, and home repairs.

Just as the state increased its provision of child care for the very young, Ohio has increased its care for the very old and infirm, in particular those with Alzheimer's disease. (A viral killer with symptoms identical to senile dementia, the disease first strips its victims of memory.) Caregivers need respite, whether for a rest break or time to run errands, and get it from the Department of Aging's Alzheimer's Respite Care Program. Temporary care is funded by the state, either in-home at or a residential facility. About 425 people had utilized the service by 1998, when the amount of money available for the care was doubled. Help for the loved ones of Alzheimer's patients is also provided via an Alzheimer's Helpline, a partnership between the Department of Aging and the Ohio Council of Alzheimer's Associations. The statewide toll-free number, which has tallied more than nine thousand calls since its 1993 inception, connects the caller with the nearest Alzheimer's chapter. Though Ohio was the second state in the nation with such a helpline, it is the first state to provide direct links with a local Alzheimer's chapter.

Also new in the Department of Aging is the First Lady's Award for Elder Caregiving, an annual presentation to someone who has devoted his or her time and effort to help an ailing friend or relative. The purpose of the award, beyond honoring one selfless person, is to increase awareness of the difficulty of caring for the elderly outside institutions.

The departments of Aging and Insurance entered a partnership in 1992 to provide counseling to senior citizens on health insurance details. Known as the Ohio Senior Health Insurance Information Program (OSHIP), the educational endeavor selects volunteers who work one-on-one with senior citizens to help them understand the complexities of health insurance. Whether the tutoring was in-person or via the toll-free telephone number, thirty thousand older Ohioans have benefited from OSHIP in its six years of existence. A different toll-free telephone number can be dialed for the service called Benefits Eligibility Screening Service (BESS). Begun in 1993, BESS lets senior citizens access information on their individual eligibility for state and federal services quickly and comprehensively. Ohio was the first state to offer such information free via telephone.

Older Ohioans also have two programs that let them help one another. RSVP volunteers assist with such services as delivering meals and working in nursing homes. The Senior Companion Program pairs up older people who can lend an ear or just chat. The Seniors Teaching and Reaching Students (STARS) program, mentioned in Chapter 4, is not the only intergenerational program under the aegis of the Department of Aging. The Foster Grandparents program matches people old enough to be grandparents with at-risk children for twenty hours per week in a relationship modeled on the real thing. Governor Voinovich praised it in the 1995 Inaugural Address. "I call it the love factor. It helps the kids, but it also brings new meaning to life for older Ohioans. I hope more of you can participate in these intergenerational programs. There is an old saying that those who bring sunshine into the lives of others cannot keep it from themselves."

"There is an old saying that those who bring sunshine into the lives of others cannot keep it from themselves."

PROTECTING OHIO'S ENVIRONMENT—
WATER, AIR, AND LAND

The Ohio Environmental Protection Agency (EPA) works to prevent and correct pollution of Ohio's water, air, and land. Because EPA's funding shortfall was hindering its ability to protect Ohio's citizens when Governor Voinovich took office, he supported more than doubling EPA's budget, from $69 million in 1991 to $149 million in 1998. Furthermore, EPA's emphasis on pollution prevention has yielded double benefits from the doubled budget—a cleaner environment without hampering economic development.

Water
Many of EPA's achievements during the Voinovich administration are due in large part to the governor's persuading the federal government to let Ohio paddle its own canoe in environmental waters. One expensive federal yacht the governor commandeered was the Safe Drinking Water Act. Leading the state and local government coalition in 1996, Governor Voinovich lobbied Congress to rewrite the nation's drinking water laws. In essence, the federal dictates lacked flexibility, costing the states money. For example, the federal rules arbitrarily added new chemicals (documentation of prior presence in drinking water notwithstanding) to the ever-lengthening list that states must look for in their water supplies with ever costlier analysis procedures. Under the new law, EPA predicts that Ohio's water providers will save more than $8 million just in monitoring costs. More savings are likely to accrue because the United States Environmental Protection Agency (USEPA) will focus on documented sources of pollution, while Ohio EPA's focus shifts to prevention— attacking contamination at the source of water intake instead of relying solely on filtering in the pipe. The new federal legislation also provides grants for loans to states at below-market interest rates for improvements to public water systems. Ohio's share by 1998 was $43 million, bringing the total available to communities across Ohio to $90 million when state funds are added.

On the home front, the governor acted to remedy Ohio EPA's funding shortfall for monitoring more than four thousand public drinking water systems. By imposing a fee on the systems, enough money was raised to detect potential health problems and ensure safe drinking water. As for meeting regulations, the compliance with the nitrate standard rose from 59 percent in 1994 to 87 percent in 1996 at public drinking water systems inspected by Ohio EPA.

Drinking water isn't the only water protected by the state. Nature blessed Ohio with abundant surface water—Lake Erie, the beautiful Ohio River, 29,000 miles of other rivers and streams and 450 lakes and ponds. Governor Voinovich worked in Washington and at home to protect Lake Erie from pollution. As chairman of the Council of Great Lakes Governors, he commissioned a study in 1993 in order to demonstrate that USEPA regulations were unnecessarily costly. By 1995 the USEPA compromised with the Great Lakes states in a less costly version of the Great Lakes Water Quality Initiative to reduce toxicity. Ohio EPA reports that the new federal rules permit innovations in preventing toxic substances from entering Lake Erie, and at costs savings to some lakefront cities. The precise figures from Ohio EPA report total savings of $136,000 annually to Ohio municipalities in the Lake Erie basin under the compromise water quality initiative. A federal master plan to protect the lake was also started in 1994. The Lakewide Management Plan (LAMP) involves citizen, business, and government leaders in a public-private partnership to develop strategies to maintain Lake Erie as a recreation source as well as a drinking water supply.

Back home in Ohio, the governor established the Lake Erie Office in Toledo to monitor lake protection up close. To pay for it, he pushed the legislature to approve sales of a Lake Erie license plate. More than 234,000 Ohioans have bought the plate that features the Marblehead Lighthouse, pouring $3.5 million into the Lake Erie Protection Fund since 1992. Governor Voinovich issued a Lake Erie report card in 1998—the first—which serves a diagnostic function in establishing benchmarks for measuring future improvements.

Ohio EPA also protected the state's water sources by developing a Watershed Management Unit, which guides twenty-five local watershed organizations in their search for remedies of water pollution from sources difficult to localize. Termed "nonpoint sources," examples are agricultural runoff, municipal sewer overflows, and industrial wastewater. Since 1992, the state has also provided financial incentives to potential polluters to urge them to find ways to keep polluted runoff from reaching streams and lakes. Among the tactics the state suggests and supports are restoring wetlands, installing sediment basins, protecting streambanks, controlling erosion, funding educational seminars, and demonstrating projects that work. One example of a financial incentive to reduce water pollution is Ohio's low-interest loans to farmers for improving conservation practices.

Of course clean water is important beyond its potability value. Both fish and people swim in it. The Voinovich administration was the first to direct General Revenue Funds for testing fish tissue. Nearly $2 million has been spent taking and analyzing samples from sport fish. Swimming standards improved, too, with a 16 percent increase in the number of miles of streams and rivers that met swimming standards in Ohio during the Voinovich administration.

Air

Ohio's air is the cleanest it has been in twenty-five years due to a combination of factors. While the federal Clean Air Act and cleaner gasoline surely had an impact in reducing air pollution, Ohio EPA employed its own innovations to help account for the fresher air over Ohio. In granting permits, Ohio EPA holds permit-seekers to an ever rising standard. That is, an innovation in technology that results in measurably cleaner air then becomes the standard that subsequent operators must meet. Ohio EPA also provides technical assistance, loans, and tightened regulations in a prevention package aimed to reduce air pollution. While motorists in Ohio may never be required to master the intricacies of toxic chemicals, many are well acquainted with one air quality safeguard—the automobile emission check, or e-check. Levels of carbon dioxide, lead, and particulate matter in the air all decreased between 1991 and 1998 in Ohio. Toxic chemicals in the air over Ohio dropped from 381 million pounds in 1987 to 144 million pounds by 1996. Between 1994 and 1995 alone, levels of sulfur dioxide dropped more than 34 percent. When Governor Voinovich took office, virtually every major urban area in Ohio failed to meet federal smog standards. By the time he left office, smog levels were so diminished that every Ohio city had passed federal muster.

Governor Voinovich took one action that reduced smog in Ohio in amounts that may never be measured. In a 1993 executive order, the governor banned smoking in all state buildings. He had read the results of the latest study on second-hand smoke, which was fingered as the culprit in about three thousand deaths per year nationwide. Exempt were residential areas of such state buildings as universities and institutions.

Land

Back on land, another national environmental issue was tackled by Governor Voinovich when he supported legislation that would give states the authority to restrict waste from entering Ohio to be dumped. As he said in the 1991 State of the State Address, "We must also act to curb the flow of out-of-state waste to and through Ohio, as well as to better control the production and disposal of hazardous materials and toxic waste." In a bilateral move, he signed an agreement with the state of New Jersey to crack down on illegal admissions of solid waste from New Jersey to Ohio. In fact, he established a new EPA division to handle such issues, called the Division of Solid and Infectious Waste Management. Hazardous Waste remained a separate division. The governor made good on the pledge to keep Ohio from being a dumping ground for hazardous waste by proposing a moratorium on hazardous waste incinerators. A three-year ban went into effect in 1992. In 1997 the Ohio EPA director took steps to continue the ban for at least three more years.

As for solid waste generated by Ohioans, the governor proposed a fee on solid waste disposal in 1993 to ensure that landfills were constructed and operated safely. The fee generated money for more inspectors, now numbering thirty. In 1993 there were only ten inspectors for the entire state.

What goes on underground got the attention of the Ohio EPA during the Voinovich years as well. The governor signed a bill that gave the EPA more muscle in monitoring liquid waste, much of it hazardous, that is injected into fifteen deepwells. The same bill gave the EPA authority to require seismic surveys to detect faults near deepwells, to force automatic shutdown in the event of a problem and to establish competence requirements for operators.

When it comes to meeting various standards for clean water, air, and land, smaller businesses and facilities are at a distinct disadvantage. Environmental rules apply to such companies as dry-cleaners, paint shops, and printers as well as to industrial giants with smokestacks. That's why the Ohio EPA, with encouragement from Governor Voinovich, developed programs especially designed to meet the compliance needs of small and mid-sized companies. The aid comes in the form of guidance through the maze of regulatory requirements and loans from a $10 million revolving fund created in 1994 by Governor Voinovich to help businesses install cleaner technologies.

While smaller businesses were offered a helping hand, Governor Voinovich challenged Ohio's one hundred most voluminous polluters to reduce their emissions of toxic gases, liquids, and solid waste above and beyond the levels required by law. Through the program called Ohio Prevention First, more than 160 Ohio companies (including 82 of the top 100 polluters) reduced emissions to the environment. According to Ohio EPA documents, the reductions total 651,000 tons of hazardous waste, 229,000 tons of solid waste, and 135 million pounds of toxics. Begun in 1993, Ohio Prevention First won an award for environmental innovation in 1997 from the Council of State Governments. In addition to the proactive approach to the worst polluters, the Ohio EPA offers technical assistance in pollution prevention plans to any company, organization or individual via its Office of Pollution Prevention, established in 1993.

One of the recommendations of Governor Voinovich's Operations

Improvement Task Force had been to improve energy efficiency, not only to save money but also to save environmental resources. Beginning in 1993, Ohio EPA guided the conversion to energy-efficient lighting in the state's buildings through the federal Green Lights program, a switch that will save $4 million annually by EPA estimates. Ohio EPA won other converts to Green Lights by offering technical assistance. By 1998, 106 Ohio corporations, plus universities, hospitals, and other nonprofit institutions had joined the energy-saving program.

Cleanup

In addition to preventing pollution, the Ohio EPA deals with the fallout from past pollution. In the 1994 State of the State Address, Governor Voinovich insisted, "We must take action early in 1994 on Senate Bill 221 [Brownfields Cleanup] to help our major urban centers in cleaning up environmentally unsafe and abandoned industrial sites and recycling them to produce jobs for our inner city residents." Passage of the legislation was high on the governor's agenda for two important reasons: environmental and economic. Cleaning up contaminated and unsightly property is of course an environmental imperative. But the locations of the brownfields—in urban areas desperate for jobs—posed an economic imperative that called for statesmanship. The resulting Voluntary Action Program (VAP) of the bill allows cleanup tailored to the eventual use of the property, a reduction in expensive administrative oversight, and long-term liability protection for present and future property owners. Because cleaning up hazardous substances is still expensive even under Ohio's streamlined procedures, Governor Voinovich insisted on a package of financial incentives—tax credits and abatements, low-interest loans and grants—to make cleanup and redevelopment economically feasible to volunteers.

Under the Voluntary Action Program, hundreds of potential volunteers are investigating property, assessing cleanup costs, and converting unproductive sites to economic rebirth. The Southern Ohio

Port Authority, for example, used the VAP to clean up an abandoned steel mill in New Boston, Ohio, which generated one hundred new jobs in Southern Ohio. A vacant nineteen-acre site in Brooklyn, Ohio, is en route via VAP to becoming a commercial shopping center. In Lockland, Ohio, a brownfield property redeveloped with VAP assistance will create up to 250 jobs. All told, more than 1,500 Ohioans have jobs as a direct result of environmental cleanup at forty sites that have completed the program.

In a related proposal, the governor signed a bill in 1994 that requires the disposal or sale of hazardous materials before a facility ceases operations. Companies must also devise security measures to prevent vandalism after shutdown. Elsewhere in cleanup efforts, Ohio is purging its landscape of scrap tires in legislation signed by the governor that created a fund to clean up existing scrap tire stockpiles and to ensure that scrap tires in the future would not be discarded on Ohio's landscape. Two mammoth piles of scrap tires were eliminated in 1997 when the Ohio EPA took over cleanup efforts of more than five million tires in two counties. More cleanups are underway.

Environmental damage caused at federal facilities should be the cleanup responsibility of the federal government, says Governor Voinovich. The new EPA Office of Federal Facilities Oversight went into action in 1994 to oversee cleanup at federal sites in Ohio—using several million dollars from the U.S. departments of Energy and Defense. Among the better known sites are the Fernald uranium processing plant near Cincinnati, the Mound Facility in Dayton, Portsmouth Gaseous Diffusion Plant at Piketon, and Wright Patterson Air Force Base in Dayton.

The governor formally announced his vision to keep Ohio beautiful in his first state of the environment address, made paddle-in-hand while floating in a canoe on the scenic Hocking River near Logan, Ohio. But the vision had taken shape almost thirty years earlier, when George Voinovich served as the architect of the Ohio Environmental Protection Agency while a member of the Ohio General

Assembly. By the 1998 State of the State Address, Governor Voinovich could report: "With respect to our environment, Ohio's air and water are the cleanest they've been in 25 years. Ohio is a national leader in voluntary efforts by business to prevent pollution and in acting to clean up polluted, urban brownfield sites. And just last year, our state park system was rated America's best. But maybe the most inspiring sign of our healthy environment is the return of the bald eagle to Ohio's skies. Today the number of eagles that nest in Ohio is the highest it's been in a half-century."

"Ohio's air and water are the cleanest they've been in twenty-five years."

PROTECTING OHIO'S NATURAL RESOURCES

Closely related to Ohio EPA's surveillance of the environment is the Department of Natural Resources' (ODNR) vigilance in maintaining balance between preservation and use of Ohio's land and water and in safeguarding plants and animals within the state's habitats. While the EPA's science is predominantly chemistry, ODNR's sciences are biology and geology. As stewards of what nature hath wrought, ODNR manages Ohio's resources through 73 state parks, 19 state forests, 113 nature preserves, and 80 wildlife areas.

ODNR's fourteen-division infrastructure got a hike in funds in 1993 when voters approved Governor Voinovich's Parks and Natural Resources Bond Issue to provide stable funding for renovation and improvement projects. How best to manage the $200 million infusion across five years was established by *NatureWorks*, the ODNR program that prioritized and oversaw the projects beginning in 1993. Completed by 1998 were hundreds of projects, such as campground improvements at Mohican State Park, rehabilitation of the Marietta State Nursery, renovation of the Muskingum River Lock No. 10 at Zanesville, and three construction projects—a major new section of the Little Miami Bikeway, the spillway at Grand Lake St. Marys, and a boardwalk at Johnson Woods Nature Preserve at Zanesville. Underway by 1998 were water system improvements at Lake Hope State Park, renovations to Salt Fork Lodge, expansion at Maumee Bay Lodge, and trail improvements at Blackhand Gorge Nature Preserve.

Despite the need for renovations, Ohio's state parks are well managed by ODNR, as recognized in 1997 by the National Gold Medal Award for parks and recreation excellence, presented to the nation's best state park program. The award, cosponsored by the National Recreation and Park Association (NRPA) and the National Sporting Goods Association, was not just a first for Ohio, but the first such award given in the NRPA's thirty-two-year history.

One reason the voters endorsed the 1994 parks and natural resources bond issue was its matching grant feature, by which local communities share the wealth for their own park and recreation projects ($44 million worth). Additional grant money uses are to increase boat access to Lake Erie and the Ohio River and for stream protection in partnership with local soil and water conservation districts. Streambank protection, the conservation education that accompanies it, and promotion of no-till framing have been increased during the Voinovich administration with *NatureWorks* grant money. ODNR estimates that soil erosion has been reduced by 75 to 80 percent, in large part because farmers have been converting to the no-till cultivation method that loosens less soil for possible erosion into streams, rivers, and lakes. Streambank protection *per se* has increased, too. Since 1996 an additional two thousand acres of stream corridors have come under the guardianship of ODNR's Division of Soil & Water Conservation, in partnership with the federal Wetland Reserve Program and local property owners. The other forty-nine states have put only half that much acreage under protection since 1996. At the end of the Voinovich administration, ODNR was managing nearly seven thousand acres of streamside corridors.

The largest recreation area in Ohio is of course Lake Erie, 2.25 million acres of which are managed by ODNR. In 1996 the department spent a year devising a strategic plan for Lake Erie's coastal resources that utilizes ODNR's expertise in research, monitoring, management, and enforcement to protect the coast. A key feature of the action plan is cooperation between state and local governments to prevent erosion, the lake's most serious threat. A byproduct of the program was that it positioned Ohio to seek and get $2 million in federal money for the various ODNR efforts to protect the lake—monitoring coastal development, habitat, wetlands, fish, and wildlife.

Another initiative of the Voinovich administration was the TreeSource program of reforestation with its goal of planting 15 million new trees each year in Ohio, up from the 10 million planted in 1990. Volunteers planted more trees in their communities, and state foresters planted more trees along the highways. Thus the goal was met, bringing Ohio's forest cover to 30 percent, up from a pre–World War II level of 12 percent, according to the U.S. Forest Service. Tree planting became an urban phenomenon as well in Ohio through its participation in the Tree City USA program. Ohio has led all other states in the number of communities qualifying for the Tree City USA designation for fifteen years, but in 1997 a new achievement was reached —208 communities in Ohio attained the Tree City USA distinction within one year, the first state to surpass the 200-community benchmark.

Increasing the amount of protected territory was another ODNR achievement during the Voinovich administration. Fifteen new nature preserves were added to ODNR's statewide system. In fact, the amount of preserve acreage owned by the ODNR Division of Natural Areas and Preserves has increased 17 percent since 1991. Ownership of non-preserve acreage has increased at more significant levels. Since 1991 more than 68,000 acres have been purchased by ODNR's Division of Wildlife, which represents a 65 percent increase in its holdings. One real estate purchase made with *NatureWorks* money was one of the largest remaining old-growth forests in Ohio, Lawrence Woods in Hardin County. Another coup was setting aside a forty-seven-mile stretch of the Kokosing River in Knox and Coshocton counties as a State Scenic River in 1997, the first such designation since 1984. Governor Voinovich, who had sponsored the scenic rivers legislation in the 1960s, was present for the formal designation of the Kokosing. Support for Ohio's scenic rivers is funded in part by proceeds from sales of a commemorative license plate initiated by ODNR in 1995 that has generated half a million dollars.

Protecting habitats is one reason Ohio has chronicled so many achievements in restoring endangered species. Through a variety of partnerships with other government agencies, outdoor sporting organizations, environmental groups and private businesses, ODNR launched new programs in the 1990s to reverse declines of certain species, to reestablish species that had disappeared from Ohio and to protect their habitats. Two species that had not lived in Ohio for decades were escorted back in 1996 by ODNR Division of Wildlife biologists—trumpeter swans in selected wetlands and ospreys at five locations near bodies of water. Species whose declines were reversed include bald eagles, river otters, and wild turkeys. One bird species coaxed into nesting in Ohio was formerly just a perennial flyover— the peregrine falcon. ODNR also supplied the numbers to document the governor's quote about the proliferation of bald eagles. In 1998, 47 eagle parents produced 48 eaglets, compared to 12 newborn eagles in 1991. Wildlife, like scenic rivers and Lake Erie, has benefited in Ohio from the sale of special license plates. Introduced as late as November 1997, the license plates generated $377,000 for the Wildlife and Endangered Species Protection Fund in one year.

Recycling is promoted by the Voinovich administration by formal action as well as by words. In an ODNR program called *Recycle, Ohio!* which was begun in 1991, state agencies are reducing waste, increasing recycling, and buying more products made of recycled materials. When the state's 36,000 employees recycle, the landscape notices. In FY 1996, for example, more than 7,300,000 pounds of materials were recycled by state agencies—enough to make a mountain of paper, cardboard, metals, glass, plastic, and food compost that would hide the Statehouse. Another action to encourage reduce-reuse-recyle behavior was the distribution of $7.5 million in FY 1998 to local governments for recycling, litter prevention, and community beautification. The state's lead in recycling and using recycled products was noticed by at least one industry publication. *Waste Age/ Recycling Times* lists Ohio as sixth best in the nation as a recycler, and a voluntary one at that. The magazine's study reported that 34 percent of Ohio's industrial, commercial, and residential waste is turned over for possible reincarnation in other uses.

A mountain of recyclables does no good unless the transformed versions are purchased. That's why ODNR formed a partnership with twelve businesses to create the Ohio Buy Recycled Alliance. Begun as a pilot project in Cleveland in 1995, the alliance is now a statewide network of 140 members, including some of Ohio's largest corporations, all of which purchase items made from recyclables and encourage other businesses to do the same. Meanwhile, the Voinovich administration started tracking purchases of products made from recycled components. Numbers from ODNR for FY 1996 show that the state spent $7.6 million on supplies made from material that had a former life, a 27 percent increase in one year. Specific examples of these purchases are paper and office supplies, recyclable loading pallets, and remodeling materials.

PROTECTING THE HEALTH OF OHIOANS

New programs to keep Ohioans healthier during the administration of Governor Voinovich were not restricted to the broad oversight of *Ohio Families and Children First*. Within the Department of Health, one such initiative was the Childhood Lead Poisoning Prevention Program, funded by federal grants via the Centers for Disease Control. The federal dollars increased after 1994 when Ohio passed a lead poisoning prevention law that required mandatory reporting of lead hazards and the licensing of lead inspectors.

Lead poisoning can occur through ingestion, inhalation, or absorption through the skin. Because lead in a human's system can damage the brain, kidneys, liver, and other organs, locating lead sources and finding children who have been exposed to lead are the two major tactics of prevention strategy. The program targets children under the age of three. Specific efforts include blood screening of children, identification of sources of lead in homes of the target group (usually paint in older buildings), community education, surveillance, and case management. Health officials also shifted their focus to high-risk zip code areas, those that meet one of the following criteria: (1) at least 27 percent of the housing was built before 1950, or (2) at least 12 percent of the children under age thirty-five months who were screened in the prior calendar year had elevated lead levels in their blood. Data from the Department of Health show that 80,455 children were screened in FY 1996. Of those, 10.4 percent had high lead levels. The next year, 105,948 children were screened, with 8.4 percent showing high lead levels. In those two years, 3,285 homes of lead-poisoned children were inspected for lead hazards.

Another of Governor Voinovich's ideas is intended to increase the number of physicians in areas that need more doctors. The Physician Loan Repayment Program, now in its fourth year, permits educational loans up to $20,000 to medical students. In exchange, the future doctors pledge to work in a public agency in one of Ohio's sixty medically underserved areas. Since the opportunity began, twenty-two physicians have graduated and begun practice in primary care. Simple math suggests that these doctors cumulatively will see thousands of patients each year.

One of the more overt efforts to improve quality during the Voinovich administration occurred in the Department of Health with the Ohio Public Health Leadership Institute (OPHLI) to increase the number of community leaders who understand health issues. Launched in 1994 with funds from the Centers for Disease Control and the National Association of County and City Health Officials, the program puts together groups of health experts and local leaders who work as teams to solve local health problems.

A second change that puts Ohio in a leadership position in health delivery is its redesign of measures of quality for six types of outpatient care facilities (such as birthing centers) and for nine types of frequently used procedures (such as open-heart surgery). Integrated into traditional measures of staff-to-patient ratios and facility capacity was an assessment of patients' health outcomes. The new quality assurance system, which began in Ohio's metropolitan areas in 1996, took effect in rural areas in 1997.

A third health leadership initiative was the Office of Women's Health, also begun in 1994, which surveys issues pertinent to women and recommends actions, such as legislation or policy development. Among the achievements of the office was hosting a national conference, "Toward the Year 2000: Improving Women's Health in Ohio," and compiling the results of statewide focus groups into a booklet titled "Women's Data Chartbook." Ohio is one of only four states to establish an office devoted to women's health matters.

During Governor Voinovich's tenure the Department of Health undertook a major inventory of health resources, including personnel, facilities, and equipment. The information gathered was then categorized by county so that profiles are now available for the state as well as for each county for policy planners to use as references. A companion study was done in early 1998 called the Ohio Family Health Survey to obtain baseline data on the health picture of Ohioans. Facts and opinions were collected on sources of health care coverage, health care benefits, reasons for lack of insurance, access to care, level of satisfaction with care, and general health status. Also new in the 1990s was the Ohio Public Health Plan, a policy shift to position health departments for a more businesslike approach to their functions.

The Department of Health stepped up its battle against cancer starting in January 1992 with the Ohio Cancer Incidence Surveillance System (CISS). Every newly diagnosed case of cancer in the state must be reported to the department in order to learn which populations are most at-risk for various cancers. In the last year for which data were available from the Department of Health, FY 1996, Ohio hospitals and physicians in private practice reported 52,000 new cases of cancer. The information is shared with a host of health organizations, all of which are engaged in improving prevention and early detection efforts.

Early detection and treatment are the goals of the Ohio campaign against breast and cervical cancer, which are easier to cure when caught early. Using grants from the Centers for Disease Control, the Department of Health launched statewide services in 1995 through twelve regional centers in the state. The Breast and Cervical Cancer Project (BCCP) provides education, free screenings, and diagnostic services for eligible women. More than four hundred health care providers participate in screenings and treatments. In FY 1997 about ten thousand women took advantage of the screenings for the cancers. Volunteer efforts in cooperation with BCCP reach thousands more. Ohio's staunchest advocate for awareness about screenings for breast and cervical cancer is First Lady Janet Voinovich, who spearheaded the passage of legislation designating the third Thursday in October as Ohio Mammography Day. The Breast and Cervical Cancer Coalition recognized Mrs. Voinovich's work by naming an award in her honor.

One additional protection was a change in state law to require insurers to cover mammograms and PAP smears. Some of the project funding also provides medical schools with the latest detection information and data. Persons with HIV (Human Immune deficiency Virus) or AIDS (Acquired Immune Deficiency Syndrome) get medication, nursing visits, and assistance with insurance coverage through the AIDS Client Resources Section. The programs help more than four thousand AIDS patients and their families each year.

The Tobacco Risk Reduction Program in the two departments of Health and Alcohol and Drug Addiction Services got a boost from the Centers for Disease Control with grants in the amount of $263,000 per year from 1994 through 1997. One objective was to reduce the number of merchants selling tobacco products to minors by making unannounced inspection visits to vendors. About 10 percent of the state's licensed tobacco vendors were inspected by 1997, a sample large enough for generalizing trends. Data from the departments show that the number of merchants who sold tobacco items to youth was 43 percent in FY 1994 and 24 percent in FY 1997. A second objective was to reduce smoking by pregnant women. That pilot project has been expanded through a partnership with the March of Dimes. A third front against tobacco use was opened in 1997 when the campaign called Tobacco-Free Ohio was created in partnership with the American Heart Association, the American Cancer Society, and the American Lung Association with grants from a private foundation. A fourth anti-tobacco action, already mentioned, was Governor Voinovich's ban on smoking in state buildings in 1991.

Three other programs related to the health of Ohioans were initiated by the Department of Health after 1991.

1. The OPTIONS program, in conjunction with the Ohio Dental Association, matches low-income or disabled people with dentists who provide free or discounted dental care. Begun as a pilot project in 1997 with federal and private grants, OPTIONS was expanded statewide with General Revenue Fund money the next year.

2. In a program called Operation Baby Buckle, vouchers are distributed to eligible families to exchange for infant car seats. In partnership with Wal-Mart and the Safe America Foundation, the Department of Health implemented the idea in 1997. By the end of 1998 the department estimated that 3,500 free car seats will carry little Ohioans whose folks used the vouchers.

3. The health of moms and newborns was the motive for lobbying against drive-through deliveries in Ohio. In 1996, with strong support from the governor, various Ohio health agencies sought and got legislation that lets mothers and babies remain in the hospital—with insurance coverage—for at least forty-eight hours after a regular delivery and at least ninety-six hours after surgical delivery.

Other health legislation aimed to eliminate Medicare fraud by health providers. Ohio was one of the first states to ban balance billing, a practice that allowed some providers to bill patients for services and supplies above the amounts approved by Medicare standards. The ban helped curb soaring costs of Part B Supplements for millions of Ohio Medicare participants. The Department of Health set up a complaint hotline after the 1993 law was enacted so that patients could report suspected balance billing. Reports poured in at first. Dozens of investigations later, the number of complaints is declining, probably due in part to the extensive information campaign to alert seniors about the illegal billing practice and to urge them to report it. Thousands of copies of a brochure explaining balance billing and its illegality have been distributed in conjunction with the Department of Aging's OSHIP program. Although the initial version of the law extended protection to seniors at or below 600 percent of the federal poverty level, a 1995 revision extended the protection against balance billing to all Medicare beneficiaries.

GuardCare provides preventive health services in medically underserved areas by sending Ohio Army and Air National Guard medical unit members into a different county each year to assist the local health department and local service providers with free screenings. Their health list includes height, weight, blood pressure, and other vital signs; dental exams; hearing and vision screenings; screenings for lead in the blood; immunizations; blood sugar and cholesterol screenings; full blood count; electrocardiograms; and physical exams by military physicians. Referrals and follow-up care are then provided for those whose tests indicate that treatment is needed. The Adjutant General's Department reported that 943 people have been poked, pricked, and probed at GuardCare events since 1996.

The cats, dogs, and other pets of Ohioans may be safer, too, thanks to an ingenious plan by the three state departments of Health, Natural Resources, and Agriculture to halt the spread of rabies carried by raccoons. The Centers for Disease Control had warned that the rabies might become an epidemic. More than a third of a million baits containing oral rabies vaccine were dropped by air and strewn by automobile in raccoon habitats in northeast Ohio during the fall and spring of 1997. Curing creatures of the disease in the wild was supplemented by more traditional approaches—public awareness education, encouraging rabies vaccinations of cats and dogs, and surveillance of the usual suspects.

The Livestock Show Reform Act was the culmination of the Department of Agriculture efforts to halt the adulteration of livestock —not just for the safety of the animals, but for the health of the people who would eventually eat them. Precipitating the department's lobbying effort for the new law was the fact that eight animals on exhibit at the 1994 Ohio State Fair had tested positive for illegal drugs or vegetable oil (injected to make the animals look glossier and healthier). The department obtained convictions, began a new livestock testing program, started a statewide education program for exhibitors, and drafted what became the Livestock Show Reform Act, which was recommended to other states by the national Council of State Governments as model legislation.

PROTECTING OHIOANS FROM CRIME

Department of Rehabilitation and Correction (DRC)
Governor Voinovich summarized Ohio's prison problem in the 1993 State of the State Address as a "continuing drain on Ohio's resources, both human and financial. The budget for our adult prison system has grown by 280 percent in the last ten years, and our juvenile system, 58 percent—each triggered by unrelenting increases in our institutional population." His solution sought to balance the need for longer sentences for serious and repeat offenders with community-based punishments and alternatives to incarceration for lesser offenders. Furthermore, under the new approach, research would govern decisions on what punishments best fit which crimes and on which prisoners to release. The philosophy emerged in a package of bills and initiatives—Cornerstones for Corrections, Truth in Sentencing

legislation (Senate Bill 2), and a revision of Ohio Parole Board release guidelines.

Expanding prison capacity was one response to the unrelenting increases in the institutional population. Since 1991, 10,063 prison beds have been added, with 5,265 planned or under construction. Legislation at the end of December 1998 will provide funding for another 1,250 beds. The DRC construction project that garnered the most attention in the 1990s was the new maximum-security Ohio State Penitentiary in Youngstown. Opened in 1998 with state-of-the-art security devices, the 500-bed Supermax is the most secure of Ohio's prisons. Following the damage to the Southern Ohio Correctional Facility during the 1993 riot at Lucasville, that prison was rebuilt and upgraded with state-of-the-art security equipment.

Efforts more far-reaching than reconstruction emerged in the aftermath of the Lucasville riot. DRC adopted critical incident management methods to prevent riots and to stand ready to control disturbances should they occur. The safety of staff and inmates was bolstered by a prison search program called Operation Clearout and by fielding tactical units that can respond quickly to a variety of challenges. Another development was a Zero Tolerance approach to drug use in prisons. Because the improvements could not be accomplished without additional personnel, the DRC staff total grew from 8,700 in 1991 to 15,000 in 1998, counterbalancing the 16.5 percent reduction in other state agencies that the governor had effected.

In seeking alternatives to locking up lawbreakers, state officials have provided funds, advice, technical support, and training for community-based correctional facilities, halfway houses, and alternative sentencing programs. Two examples of the less restrictive alternative sentencing are electronic monitoring and probation with check-in. Total spent on these alternatives since 1991 is $277 million. The DRC estimated that non-prison punishments were meted out to 72,500 individuals between 1991 and 1998.

New parole guidelines, implemented by the Ohio Parole Board in 1998, employ an instrument that has been scientifically tested for validity and reliability in predicting which inmates pose safety risks. In addition to the prediction instrument, DRC reviewed policies and procedures related to parole, increased its use of technology, forged more local partnerships and pursued national accreditation for parole field services. In a first for Ohio's DRC, the American Correctional Association awarded accreditation to Ohio's Parole Board and Adult Parole Authority in 1995. More significant was the announcement in November 1998 that Ohio now has the first fully accredited department of corrections in the nation. Conferred by the American Correctional Association, the distinction certifies that every facet of Ohio's DRC meets rigorous accreditation standards.

DRC works in partnership with other state agencies to provide treatment for inmates with substance abuse problems or mental health diagnoses. Since 1991 DRC has worked with the Department of Alcohol and Drug Addiction Services to provide services to the estimated 80 percent of the prison population who have abused alcohol or drugs. Ohio's range of services—drug testing, interdiction, sanctions, and treatment—was implemented before it was required by the federal government of all state prison systems. The Ohio model has been repeatedly cited by the U.S. Department of Justice as an example of excellence.

In 1995, DRC collaborated with the Department of Mental Health to provide mental health care to prisoners. Ohio was not the first state to have faced a federal class-action lawsuit alleging inadequate mental health care in prisons. Because other states had waged expensive court battles on the issue and lost, Ohio's response was to comply without a court fight when a suit was filed in 1993 (*Dunn v. Voinovich*). Several innovations have resulted from the DRC/MH partnership.

1. The Oakwood Correctional Facility was recommissioned as an acute care prison for treating inmates with mental health needs.
2. The number of acute care beds at Oakwood increased from 50 to 131.

3. Residential Treatment Units (RTUs) were set aside within other prisons for treating inmates whose needs are less acute. Piloted in Ohio, the innovative RTUs provide a full range of mental health services on an out-patient basis.

4. A cluster concept was initiated whereby a team of mental health care professionals serves groups of institutions in twelve geographic regions. The twelve teams provide assessment, evaluation, and crisis intervention as well as treatment.

One new DRC office, Victim Services, was started in 1997 to provide crisis intervention, information, and referrals to survivors of crime and their families. Staffed by crime victims and victim advocates, the office has established a network of victim services coordinators in each of the prison and parole regions throughout the state. One seat on the Ohio Parole Board has been set aside for a crime survivor, and the department has initiated mediation sessions between victims and offenders.

Despite the overall growth in expenditures for prisons and personnel to run them, DRC had compiled the following package of efficiencies by 1997. Ohio's daily cost per inmate was $42.38, which is 28 percent below the national average. Ohio has the lowest medical costs per inmate, $4.93, which is 34 percent below the national average. The cost of construction of a medium security prison bed was $22,177, which is 44 percent below the national average.

Department of Youth Services (DYS)

"I am especially proud that our benchmark RECLAIM Ohio program for juvenile corrections rolls out statewide this month. The nine pilot projects recorded a 44 percent reduction in youth incarcerations. This initiative is giving juvenile courts the flexibility to rehabilitate youthful offenders and reclaim their lives," Governor Voinovich said in the 1995 State of the State Address. RECLAIM Ohio, like the welfare reform designed by Governor Voinovich, was different because it shifted money and decision making to the county

level. County juvenile courts, all eighty-eight of which were participating in the new paradigm by 1995, use state funds to buy secure incarceration from DYS. Or, counties can use the money to develop or
expand local options, including close-to-home corrections facilities.
Instead of routinely shipping youthful offenders off to a state-run
facility, local authorities could devise corrections to fit individual
situations and to incorporate families into treatment. Figures from
Youth Services tell the story: In 1992 the total number of youth incarcerated in a DYS facility was 2,538. By 1997 the number had
dropped to under 1,900. Because Ohio had recorded a decline in
jailed youth against a backdrop of rising youth crime nationwide,
the Kennedy School of Government at Harvard University named
RECLAIM Ohio as one of the twenty-five most innovative programs in government in 1996, a mere two years after the program's
inception.

The governor called a juvenile crime summit in 1997 to prepare
Ohio to avoid the epidemic in juvenile crime that criminologists predict will occur by 2005 as the number of youth in America burgeons.
Following the juvenile crime summit, other changes were made in
the way youth entered and exited the incarceration system. A new division called the Release Authority, complete with new methods,
started operations within DYS in 1998. One member of the five-
member authority board must be a victim of juvenile crime or a victim's advocate—much like the counterpart on the Ohio Parole
Board. Also similar was the creation of the Office of Victim Services
within DYS, which informs victims of an offender's status, treatment
progress, and impending release.

The actual buildings in which youth are incarcerated underwent
substantial changes during the Voinovich administration. Though
the approach to sentencing aimed to keep more youth in their home
communities, some nevertheless landed in DYS centers. For those
male youths committed to DYS jurisdiction by any of the eighty-
eight county juvenile courts in Ohio, the first stop is now the Circleville Reception and Assessment Center. Opened for its new function

in 1996, the converted center at Circleville provides a battery of tests and assessments (such as medical and mental health exams and social history reviews) within a three-week period. Decisions are then made on which institution would be best for each youth and which programs would best prepare him for transition to the community. A companion facility for female offenders, also designated for reception and assessment, was established at Scioto in 1993 after renovation of the 1858-vintage campus.

As youth crime increased nationwide throughout the 1980s, options for housing offenders in Ohio began to decrease. To remedy the infrastructure problem, DYS created nine Community Corrections Facilities since 1991 that are available to judges in fifty-one counties as an option to sentencing youth directly to a DYS detention center. But more detention centers were needed as counties exhausted their resources for youth lockups. The Voinovich administration therefore supported a set-aside of $22.8 million in state matching dollars to create or expand eleven more detention facilities (added to the thirty-five existing centers) in FY 1997–98.

Some of the existing facilities were designated for specific populations in order to consolidate highly specialized services in one location. In 1998 DYS began construction of a new high-security facility at Marion that is scheduled for completion in 2000. A medium-security center for youth from counties south of Interstate 70 was opened near Portsmouth in 1996. For youth ages twelve to eighteen deemed medically fragile or mentally disabled, the Opportunity Center opened its doors in 1996. In addition, the Voinovich administration supported new investment for DYS health and mental health personnel, doubling their number since 1994. Juvenile male sex offenders are now housed at the Riverview Juvenile Correction Center, which completed transition to that purpose in 1997. To increase treatment for sentenced youths with alcohol or drug abuse problems, DYS designated the Mohican Youth Center as its facility for serving that population. Three institutions, and half of a fourth, were deemed beyond rehabilitation after 1994 and were closed.

Office of Criminal Justice Services (OCJS)

The state's criminal justice clearinghouse administers grants and functions as the research, policy, and program evaluation unit of crime fighting in Ohio. Operated earlier as a subsidiary of two different agencies, Criminal Justice Services was converted to an independent office in 1994, a vantage that helped the office fulfill a pledge by Governor Voinovich to improve cooperation between state and local law enforcement officials.

First step in managing that task was the development of the Criminal Justice Information System (CJIS) Improvement Plan. Like a mini-OIT, the improvement process solicited input from all levels of government and members of the criminal justice system statewide. The improved system that resulted pivots on a new governance structure comprised of an executive board, a policy board, and regional working groups, the last of which forge the lines of communication between local and state officials. As for improvements to specific functions, sixty-three tasks in the information system were flagged for improvement. Chief among these was implementation of an automated fingerprint identification system that incorporated the use of fifty-eight new electronic fingerprint scanners called Live Scans. Mayor Voinovich had implemented the automated fingerprint system in Cleveland; Governor Voinovich urged the state to adopt it, too. By late 1998, about 80 percent of the arrest reports in Ohio were being submitted electronically.

Even more revolutionary is Ohio's participation in DNA technology to identify criminals. The process provides a more accurate means of identification than fingerprinting because of the unique and precise images of DNA. In Ohio, the DNA technology was fully operational by late 1998, when local law enforcement agencies could request free searches for DNA matches in their criminal investigations through the Ohio Attorney General's Office.

Reporting of criminal and court actions was also streamlined at OCJS. State legislation clarified the reporting of criminal dispositions, and state funding permitted the implementation of automated reporting of court dispositions to the federal Bureau of Criminal Identification and Investigation, the nation's repository of criminal histories.

One of OCJS's major jobs is coordinating prevention efforts statewide through the Ohio Violence Prevention Center, established by Governor Voinovich in 1995. The Center provides information on violence prevention programs as well as media messages about violence prevention. In order to review and evaluate all the existing criminal justice programs in the state, the Center funded the Criminal Justice Program Evaluation Initiative. The initiative goes beyond evaluating *per se* and providing assistance on evaluation. Another of its functions is to share information on criminal justice programs that get good evaluations and that seem to work in preventing crime.

Among the major grants administered by OCJS since 1994 are reimbursements to county prosecutors for the costs of prosecuting felonies that occur at institutions operated by the departments of Rehabilitation and Correction and Youth Services. OCJS has also provided training for those who work in criminal justice. Expertise and technical assistance on Community Oriented Policing have been shared with several communities hoping to improve residents' involvement in reducing crime. OCJS also cohosted, with various law enforcement agencies, four conferences on Community Oriented Policing and published a guidebook on the subject. State-of-the-art investigative techniques were taught to more than three hundred narcotics officers in other OCJS-sponsored training. Criminal Justice Services was also a cosponsor of the Governor's Juvenile Crime Summits in 1997 and 1998.

The agency also promoted the use of federal surplus property in the war on drugs. Local law enforcement had access to more than $50 million worth of equipment such as night vision goggles, bulletproof vests, vehicles, camouflage clothing, helmets, and office equipment.

Department of Alcohol and
Drug Addiction Services (ODADAS)

The statistical correlation between substance abuse and crime is so compelling that ODADAS has become a partner in some of the efforts to halt crime in Ohio. The governor led the way for one innovation to prevent drug users from graduating to more serious crime through the establishment of drug courts, funded in part with federal money. In short, nonviolent offenders are placed in court-supervised treatment in a partnership between ODADAS and the Ohio Supreme Court. Drug courts have been established in twelve counties, with eight more scheduled to begin session in FY 1998.

A similar program administered by ODADAS is Treatment Alternatives to Street Crime (TASC), which goes beyond treatment for substance abuse to provide training and job search skills to nonviolent offenders. Since 1994 ODADAS has served 15,763 people through TASC and aided court decisions with 7,486 assessments. Full-service clients whose assessments result in treatment and case management number 8,277. Of those thousands served by TASC, only 4 percent have been rearrested and only 3 percent have been incarcerated. ODADAS also did its part in crime prevention through the Violence Prevention Process, a training program for anyone who faces the specter of working with addicted people prone to violence. Begun in 1991, the violence prevention training has been completed by 4,500 people.

"Today, violent crime is down, the overall crime rate is down, and Ohio is a safer place to live, work, and raise a family."

In 1997 Governor Voinovich reported in the State of the State Address on his achievements in protecting Ohioans, "Together, we made a commitment to be a better partner to local law enforcement, to enact tougher laws, to build more prisons and to put more violent criminals behind bars. Today, violent crime is down, the overall crime rate is down, and Ohio is a safer place to live, work, and raise a family."

PROTECTING OHIOANS ON
THE HIGHWAYS AND BYWAYS

During the Voinovich administration, the Department of Public Safety (DPS) reduced danger on the roads by controlling hazardous drivers in three categories: drunk drivers, road ragers, and teenagers. Deaths from alcohol-related traffic accidents in Ohio dropped from 623 in 1990 to 390 in 1997, according to DPS documents. Among the Department of Public Safety's initiatives were selective traffic enforcement, sobriety checkpoints, the Governor's Advisory Council on Impaired Driving, better partnership efforts among law enforcement agencies, and a hotline for reporting drivers with drunken symptoms—1-800-GRAB-DUI. In 1993 when a stricter driving-under-the-influence law took effect, administrative license suspensions increased for drinkers nabbed while driving. By December 1997 the Bureau of Motor Vehicles had recorded the following totals: almost 270,000 suspensions for positive test results for substances, nearly 83,000 suspensions for refusal to test, about 55,500 vehicle immobilizations, and close to 3,000 vehicles confiscated. DPS used separate programs—The Sober Truth, None for Under 21, and Cops in Shops —to curb teenage drinkers who drove. The results, according to DPS, were 46 alcohol-related traffic deaths for ages sixteen to twenty in 1997, down from 155 in 1989.

TRIAD is the acronym of the DPS program that focuses on the phenomenon the media call road rage, evidenced by violations ranging from crossing several lanes of traffic at once to brandishing weapons. Targeting Reckless, Intimidating, Aggressive Drivers, which was begun in 1997, was Ohio's response to the increase in incidences of highway violence, reported by the Automobile Association of America to have risen 51 percent between 1990 and 1995. Road rage has resulted in fatalities in Ohio's three largest cities. Forty-two TRIAD operations, using planes and helicopters as well as patrols on the ground, yielded 728 arrests in its first year, with the total by late 1998 climbing to 1,448.

Teenagers, long documented as the demographic group with the highest number of accidents, face a new graduated licensing plan in Ohio that requires more driving experience before obtaining a probationary license. At age fifteen years, six months, a teen may get a driver's permit, but then must spend more hours in driver training class and more hours in driving practice with a parent, guardian or instructor before being allowed to take the formal exam at age sixteen. Also new for teens is a restriction on the number of people in a vehicle to the number of working seat belts, which of course must be fastened. The stipulations for suspension or revocation of the license are stricter for holders of the probationary license, between ages sixteen and eighteen. Ohio was one of only six states with graduated licensing when it was implemented in 1998.

Emergency management functions in Ohio had moved to the Department of Public Safety in 1995, well enough in advance of the Spring 1997 floods for rapid response to the devastation of 6,500 residences that drove nearly 20,000 Ohioans from their homes. The new Emergency Operations Center coordinated the work of thirty-five state, federal and volunteer agencies that responded when the rains pushed rivers out of their banks in eighteen counties. Also in place was the Ohio Volunteer Organizations Active in Disasters, created in 1991, which coordinates emergency response activities of about thirty volunteer organizations from a work station at the Emergency Operations Center.

During Governor Voinovich's terms as governor, Ohio spent more money than any other state on improving railroad grade crossings, nearly $15 million per year. PUCO, ODOT, and the Ohio Railroad Development Commission worked in concert to unravel the arcana of pouncing on federal dollars to construct warning devices at grade crossings. According to PUCO documents, the number of both accidents and fatalities at railroad crossings have decreased since 1991 in Ohio. The number of accidents dropped from 325 in 1991 to 94 by early December, 1998, while the number of fatalities decreased from 56 in 1991 to 12 by December of 1998.

The Green Buckeye on gas pumps in Ohio assures Ohioans that underground storage tanks full of gasoline meet certain standards. Begun Labor Day 1997, the program was designed to let motorists know which stations were in compliance with environmental laws. A Green Buckeye means that the tanks are registered with the Department of Commerce's Bureau of Underground Storage Tank Regulation (BUSTR) and therefore use leak detection methods. Though placing the symbols was intended to reward responsible environmental practices, the stickers also signal a measure of safety to drivers pumping gasoline.

Improving the ability of volunteer fire departments to protect Ohioans is a function of the State Fire Marshal's grants. Between 1994 and 1998, those grants increased from $500,000 to $725,00, according to Commerce data. The funds are used to buy such items as protective clothing for firefighters and self-contained breathing equipment. Commerce also landed $1 million in grants in 1998 to help volunteer departments pay for mandatory training of their firefighters. One Commerce initiative probably improved the quality of life for firefighters while protecting thousands of Ohioans who love fireworks. The department helped develop new laws passed in 1997 that toughened requirements for fireworks manufacturers, distributors, and wholesalers as well as purchasers and exhibitors.

MAKING CONSUMER PROTECTION
FIT QUALITY STANDARDS

Some of the innovations during the Voinovich years had staffers working harder to help Ohioans make smarter purchases. For home buyers there was the 1993 law that created a disclosure form detailing the condition of property for sale. Managed by the Division of Real Estate in Commerce, the form must be completed by sellers in order to let buyers know about potential problems of property on the market. For investors there is the investor protection hotline, 1-800-788-1194, first answered by Commerce's Division of Securities staffers in 1997. Buyers of investments can check to see if a salesperson has a license or a disciplinary record and whether an item offered for sale is properly registered in Ohio. Investors can also phone the hotline to request complaint forms and to check the status of a complaint.

Purchasers of insurance saw several changes that aided their decision making. Broadest in scope was the 1996 compilation of a database of historical information on licensed insurers dating to the 1940s. Housed in the Department of Insurance, the information is available to other state agencies as well as to the public. In health care insurance, the department administered new laws that improved accessibility and affordability for the small employer category. The legislation also called for carriers to hold open enrollment periods for health care coverage and allowed for the formation of health care alliances. A separate law endorsed by Insurance denied the use of genetic testing in health insurance underwriting for ten years, after which a task force will report its findings to the General Assembly. Another improvement in the health insurance field was the standardization of Medicare supplemental insurance into ten plans with an open enrollment period for their purchase. For life insurance, the Department of Insurance required insurers to provide more information to potential buyers and regulated the conduct of agents selling life insurance and annuities. For homeowners in counties where underground mines could threaten property, mine subsidence insurance was made mandatory. The Department of Insurance also creates information pamphlets for consumers, all of whom need different types of insurance but few of whom have ever taken a course in the subject. The "shopper's guides" on automobile, homeowners, health, life, long-term care, and Medicare supplemental insurance are distributed free and updated annually. Since 1991 nearly one million copies of various insurance guides have been printed and distributed at such diverse locations as county fairs, public libraries, and tax-counseling centers or via mail.

One-stops for the convenience of Ohio motorists are similar to the one-stops available for construction plans and permits and job seeking and training. The goal of the Bureau of Motor Vehicles is to locate vehicle registration, vehicle titling, and driver's licensing examination as close as possible to the state's 213 deputy registrars. One-stops with at least two of the three functions have increased to 70 since 1993. One-stops with all three services number 27, up from 12 in 1993. Deputy registrars were also empowered to register new voters and update voter registrations for citizens under the Motor Voter legislation. After January 1, 1995, more than half a million eligible voters took advantage of the convenience of processing paperwork in one stop for the privileges of voting and driving. BMV even made life easier for those who had their driver's licenses suspended. Prior to 1991, the sole office that processed reinstatements was in Columbus. Ohio now has regional reinstatement centers in Cleveland, Toledo, Youngstown, Canton, and Cincinnati.

The quality of life for Ohioans with hearing and speech impairments improved in 1992 when PUCO implemented the Telecommunications Relay Service. Simply put, a third person assists in communications between an impaired person and a nonimpaired person. The impaired person sends the message in typed form (using special equipment) to a communications assistant, who then reads the message to the nonimpaired receiver. The assistant recodes the speech of the nonimpaired party into typed form for the impaired person to read—so that entire conversations can transpire between sender and receiver via the assistant. The first call over the system was placed on November 13, 1992—by Governor George V. Voinovich.

EPILOGUE

Enjoying a Head Start

"Do a good job with the job you have, and the future will take care of itself."

VOTERS WENT TO the polls Tuesday, November 3, 1998, and empowered George V. Voinovich to be the United States Senator from Ohio to succeed Senator John Glenn. Governor Voinovich amassed 56 percent of the vote, while his Democratic opponent Mary Boyle got 44 percent.

At the Republican victory celebration in Columbus, Ohio's sixty-fifth governor was surrounded by his family. Directly behind him as he made his formal remarks was the first grandchild of George and Janet Voinovich—Mary Faith Voinovich, daughter of George Voinovich, Jr., and his wife Dina. Though Mary Faith was described as the star of the governor's television advertisements during the campaign, she managed to make her toddler self the background star of the victory speech as well. Evident on the senator-elect's lapel as he stood on the stage was his mother's Thanks Badge, the highest honor a Girl Scout volunteer can receive. Another heirloom was visible around his neck—the white and blue ribbon of his father's Boy Scout Silver Beaver Medal. The red tie spangled with children was his own, the veritable fashion signature of the governor who puts family and children first.

The governor will be sworn into office as the junior senator from Ohio to Republican Mike DeWine, who had served as lieutenant governor from 1991 to 1995. Governor Voinovich did point out in his victory speech that he is "the senior citizen senator from Ohio." Age and date of election to the Senate aside, George Voinovich will not be a newcomer to senators or their politicking. Even before he was elected president of the National League of Cities in 1985, Mayor Voinovich learned and lobbied his way around Washington for a host of causes pertinent to America's major cities, including involvement in Ronald Reagan's New Federalism Initiative. His 1997–98 stint as chairman of the National Governors' Association served less as a refresher course on federal lobbying than as a degree of acknowledgment of his national leadership by state governors.

Throughout his tenure as governor of Ohio, he "had one foot in Washington," as he described his efforts to plead cases for the states before Congress and its committees and throughout the executive apparatus of the federal government. And as should be expected, he did it more cheaply—spending $435,000 to operate the State of Ohio's Washington Office, 35 percent less than the $670,000 spent in his predecessor's last year as governor.

He was the point man in challenging unfunded mandate legislation in Congress. In related battles, arguing that USEPA standards for clean air and safe drinking water were too costly and not demonstrably beneficial, he reined in bureaucrats who would wreak environmental havoc on state budgets. Governor Voinovich toiled for welfare reform, Medicaid rule exceptions in order to provide health coverage for uninsured children, and a highway bill that garnered increased federal dollars for Ohio from the Highway Trust Fund. Headlines back home matched the size of those achievements.

Known less widely were other accomplishments of the Washington

Office in securing legislation beneficial to Ohio. Though disaster relief funds are *pro forma* in crises of the magnitude of Ohio's Spring 1997 and 1998 floods, Governor Voinovich's staff was indefatigable in pushing through supplemental grants from a host of separate funds. In all, $145 million materialized for disaster relief assistance. Ohio's crew in Washington staved off changes in the formula for calculating block grant money for substance abuse prevention and mental health treatment and headed off an energy tax that would have cost thousands of Ohioans their jobs. Among the other appropriations to the credit of the Washington Office of the governor were $95 million to replace buses in regional transit authorities, $38.5 million to divide among Ohio National Guard construction projects, $4.5 million to study Lake Erie erosion, $1.6 million to research coal-fired power plants, and a third of a million dollars to research Ohio's e-check program on vehicle emissions. Beyond the halls of Congress, Governor Voinovich's Washington Office stayed busy in far-flung executive branch offices tending to myriad details that might affect Ohioans.

The point should be abundantly clear: Governor Voinovich has a head start on the Senate job. He has won seats on the Environmental and Public Works Committee and the Governmental Affairs Committee. In his victory speech he pledged to take the "working harder and smarter" philosophy from Ohio to Washington. He also said he believed in the maxim, "Do a good job with the job you have, and the future will take care of itself." He had said that before, early in his governorship. It's an heirloom ideal handed down by his father, one that frames the work ethic that is George Voinovich's legacy to the people of Ohio.

THE CABINET OF GOVERNOR GEORGE VOINOVICH, 1991–1998

Lieutenant Governor—Michael DeWine, 1991–95;
  Nancy P. Hollister, 1995–98

Adjutant General—Maj. Gen. Richard C. Alexander

Administrative Services—Stephen A. Perry, 1991–93;
  James Conrad, 1993–95; Sandra A. Drabik, 1995–98

Aging—Judith Y. Brachman

Agriculture—Fred L. Dailey

Alcohol and Drug Addiction Services—Luceille Fleming

Board of Regents—Elaine Hairston, 1991–97; Roderick Chu, 1998

Budget and Management—R. Gregory Browning, 1991–98;
  Paolo A. DeMaria, 1998

Commerce—Nancy S. Chiles Dix, 1991–94; Donna Owens, 1994–98

Development—Donald E. Jakeway, 1991–97;
  Joseph C. Robertson, 1997–98

Education—Ted Sanders, 1991–95; John M. Goff, 1995–98

Employment Services—James Conrad, 1991–93;
  Debra R. Bowland, 1993–98

Environmental Protection—Donald R. Schregardus

Health—Edward G. Kilroy, 1991–92; Pitamber Somani, 1992–97;
  William T. Ryan, Jr., 1997–98; Lou Ellen Fairless, 1998

Human Services—Terry A. Wallace, 1991–92;
James Conrad, 1992–93; Arnold R. Tompkins, 1993–98;
Wayne Sholes, 1998

Industrial Commission—Donald Colasurd, 1991–94;
Patrick Gannon, 1994–97; William E. Thompson, 1997–98

Industrial Relations—John P. Stozich, 1991–95 (Department merged
with Commerce.)

Insurance—Harold T. Duryee

Liquor Control—John R. Hall, 1991–93;
Michael A. Akrouche, 1993–97; Bill Vasil, 1997 (Department
eliminated 1997.)

Lottery Commission—Virgil Brown, 1991–95;
William G. Howell, 1995–98

Mental Health—Michael F. Hogan

Mental Retardation and Developmental Disabilities—
Jerome C. Manuel

Natural Resources—Frances S. Buchholzer, 1991–95;
Donald C. Anderson, 1995–98

Public Safety—Charles D. Shipley, 1991–97;
Mitchell J. Brown, 1997–98

Public Utilities Commission—Craig A. Glazer

Quality—Steve D. Wall (Office established 1993.)

Rehabilitation and Correction—Reginald A. Wilkinson

Taxation—Roger W. Tracy

Transportation—Jerry Wray

Workers' Compensation—Patrick Mihm, 1990–95;
William W. Pfeiffer, 1995; James Conrad, 1995–98

Youth Services—Geno J. Natalucci-Persichetti

THE SENIOR STAFF OF GOVERNOR GEORGE VOINOVICH, 1991–1998

Maria Armstrong

Rocky Black

James Burns

Timothy Cosgrove

Michael Dawson

Jeffrey DeLeone

Randy Fischer

Andrew Futey

Carrie Glaeden

Christopher Guilford

Carolyn Harper

Ted Hollingsworth

Michael Koren

David Mahanes

Mary Mertz

John Meyer

Paul Mifsud

Melanie Mitchell

Thomas Needles

Douglas Preisse

Laurel Pressler

Jacqueline Romer-Sensky

Philip Serghini

Curt Steiner

Kurtis Tunnell

Beth Waldron

Michael Watson